Charging a Hat or Coat

The story of the journey to achieve suffrage

Jean R. Lane

DEDICATION

I dedicate this book to my daughter, Stephanie M. Dahm, and to all women living today and their hopes for the future. May they continue the work of their mentors and make life better and more equitable for women at work and home.

CONTENTS

CONTINUED ...

Charging a Hat or Coat

ACKNOWLEDGMENTS

I wish to thank the following people for their help and support in getting this book finished and published by encouraging me to continue writing and giving me advice on people who could help me.

To the Decatur Public Library who graciously looked and found books which I needed to research information.

To David Eiter who patiently showed me how to use my computer and corrected mistakes when I thought I had lost my work.

To Carol Tatum who listened to my story and encouraged me to continue when I doubted if I should continue. She also gave me the name of her sister, Shirley Paceley, along with Cate Adelman, who helped me in the publishing of this book when I knew absolutely nothing.

And a special thanks to Tim Wilkerson who wrote and published books. I was always asking him for advice when he finally told me to write the book and then come back to talk. He is now longer with us but I finished the book anyway.

And to all others not knowing what I was doing and needed to work on my story and were patient when I stepped back from my usual activities.

FORWARD

Charging a Hat or Coat

Being an ex-history teacher, I would research points of information I wanted to include in my teaching. As I gained experience, I noticed that there was actually little information about women in the history book. There was the token information of Deborah Sampson who disguised herself as a man to fight in the revolution and others like Martha Washington, Clara Barton, Molly Pitcher but the information was sketchy and added more like a sidebar than detailed information.

Where were the women? They did not just exist; they were working to build this country as much as the men. When the soldiers went to fight in the wars, the women stayed home and continued where the men had left off tending the farms and businesses keeping it in operation and they prospered.

March was designated as Women's Month and I sought information to add to the curriculum and show their contributions. Research takes time especially when there is little available. Then I took some graduate courses that recognized women's history and revealed their efforts to develop our country. My interest was awakened, and I began to delve into the research.

After I left teaching, I began an in-depth research of women; I read about many women. I had no course of action only to learn about as many as I could find. There were doctors, lawyers, inventors, writers, and of course, suffragists. When I studied the suffrage period, I took notes to have information available. The more I read, the more I found to research more. I had no intention of writing anything but kept notes and wrote some to clarify to myself. As I read, I learned of how many years it took for women to achieve the right to vote and just that, nothing else. What confused me was why the suffrage amendment took so long?

And here it begins. I kept researching, taking notes, and began to write down to clarify on paper what had happened. More pages were added and soon I realized how much I had and either I stop or continue. I was unsure how people felt; I thought others might be interested in reviewing the story also. I continued writing until I reached a stopping point. I realized near the end of writing that the anniversary of the 19th amendment would occur in 2020. So, I'm finishing the story and hope you find it interesting and informative.

THE NATURE OF WOMEN - HOW THEY VIEW EACH OTHER, THE WORLD VIEW AND THE HISTORY OF THE RIGHTS OF WOMEN

Charging a Hat or Coat

A fox and a scorpion are both at a river. They need to cross; the fox can swim across but the scorpion can't so he asks the fox if he would let him ride across on his back. Knowing what the scorpion can do, the fox answers No, you will sting me. I will not do that replied the scorpion; otherwise we will both die. The fox thought hard for a while and then agreed to let him ride. The scorpion climbed on and they started across but half-way, the scorpion stung him, and the fox said "Why did you do that? Now we will both die." I can't help it said the scorpion; it's my nature".

What is the nature of women?   How do they act towards each other and how does the world view them and their position? An explanation of their nature is the starting point. This story is about women who were seeking new paths of careers and the right of suffrage. In history, women had few rights and were not independent.   This is to show the challenges they faced on the journey in that goal of suffrage and researching the length of time it took to reach that goal -1920. That would be only the right to vote not full equality; today that goal has not yet been achieved; the journey is not over!

Mary Wollstonecraft was an English philosopher and writer. She was born April 2, 1759 and died at a young age on September 10, 1797. She was raised by an abusive father. He had inherited money but lost it due to mismanagement. Angry over this he became a brutal drunkard and abused both his wife and Mary. She tried to help her mother but became tired of it and left home at age nineteen. She became a companion to someone for several years but that also wasn't to her liking; she decided to start a school with her friend Fanny and her sister Eliza. She taught herself and helped her sister escape a bad marriage. The school did well for a while but after Fanny died, she closed the school and decided to write.

She wrote <u>Thoughts on Education of Daughters</u> which she sold to a London bookseller, Joseph Johnson. Moving to London she wrote children's books, translations, essays, and reviews of anthologies. She was living in an area of progressive thinkers including Thomas Paine but in 1792 went to Paris and met an American adventurer by the name of Gilbert Imlay. They had a child together who was named Fanny, but he deserted her. Mary almost committed suicide as a result but Johnson persuaded her to come back to London.

There she returned to her writing career and eventually fell in love with William Godwin who she married and settled down. They had a child also a girl whom she named Mary. Unfortunately, at the age of thirty-eight, she died leaving her daughter to be raised by her husband. This Mary also grew up to be a writer and married the poet Percy Bysshe Shelley. The book Mary wrote was the well- known Frankenstein.

Mary Wollstonecraft wrote many books about her viewpoint. She was influenced by Jacques Rousseau, Thomas Paine, and Francois Marie Arouet Voltaire. She was aware that philosophers in Europe were discussing the rights of man but were leaving out half the population who were women. She wrote the book Vindications of the Rights of Woman in 1792 as a means of explaining woman's rights. "I do not wish them (women) to have power of man but over themselves. Women are not naturally inferior to men but appear to be only because they lack education. Many women are silly and superficial but argues that this not an innate deficiency of mind but rather because men have denied them access to education. Taught from their infancy that beauty is woman's scepter and the mind shape itself in the body. Many women are vain, ignorant. shallow, sentimental, irresponsible, childish, deceitful, prevented from dealing with men on an equal basis so they had to be deceitful."[1] Her book was one considered very important to the suffrage leaders that most had read and had a copy in their possession including Elizabeth C. Stanton and Lucretia Mott, leaders of the Seneca Falls meeting. Mary Wollstonecraft is considered as having started the birth of feminism.

Mary was a very independent woman when women were considered submissive and not encouraged to do anything other than stay home and take care of home and family. She left a bad life, studied to learn an occupation, and kept on improving her skill even though she was ostracized for her efforts. She set a standard for the coming women to follow and establish.

On the other side was the viewpoint of the rest of the world at that time. William Blackstone wrote "The husband and wife are one person in law: that is, the very being or legal existence of the woman is suspended during the marriage. . . and consolidated into that of the husband."[2] This idea was called **coverture** which meant the legal identity of a woman became her husband's. If a woman leaves her husband without cause, he may seize her and

---

[1] Vindications of the Rights of Women, p. 157, Wikipedia
[2] History of Woman Suffrage, v. 1, p. 107, William Blackstone

bring her back, for he has a right to her society which he may enforce either against himself or any other person. All her personal belongings regarding property became her husband's unless it had been secured to her. If the property is not in his possession, he can take measures to reduce it to his possession. He can then dispose of it in any way, regardless of her objections. If she has earned money during marriage, he may collect it and use the money in any way he wishes. Women married or single had no political rights whatsoever. Women were considered legally dead.

Jean Jacques Rousseau wrote in 1761 " the education of women should always be relative to men, to please, to be with us, when grown up to advise, to console us to render our lives easy and agreeable; these are the duties-of women at all times. These are the duties of women and what they should be taught in their infancy. The woman is expressly formed to please the man."[3]

Rousseau was a famous philosopher whose writings stressed freedom of the individual and equality for all men. His ideas were used in the Constitution of the United States. But to his philosophy of women, Elizabeth Cady Stanton wrote in 1881,"Weak and frivolous women have been

---

[3] Jone Johnson Lewis, Humanist Institute Thought Company
the Social Contract reference site

made so by false education, customs and conventionalism. . .Men drill all spontaneity out of women until the mass of them look and act as if they were not certain of anything."[4] She is one of the founders of the suffrage movement.

Elisabeth Cady Stanton

Most of us can relate to many types of women; there are more of us than there are men. They are family members, friends, co-workers, neighbors, club members, church members, and others. Women are a large group and should

[4] Ladies of Seneca Falls, p.281

support each other morally and physically to obtain and maintain equality but this does not always happen.

Women were not educated but taught from infancy that a woman should beautify her body to attract the man. And unfortunately, that belief still holds. Women were inferior and had to be taken care of and guided. To many women their sole ambition centers around a man making him the priority. The phrase all's fair in love and war" is totally applicable to them. How many of you know or heard of a woman who lost her husband by divorce through an affair with another woman?

There are many types of women; they are unique but also unpredictable; they are totally ambivalent or as Wollstonecraft pointed out self-centered. Over two hundred years have passed and the same is mostly true of women. Mary Wollstonecraft used the words vain, ignorant, childish, deceitful, shallow, and irresponsible. Many of these words can be used today. There are many minds in the world and women delineate many of those minds. Women are competitive in the job market and for men. That means there is no support for each other only an adversary who needs to be eliminated. Women can be jealous or envious of you if you have something or do something that they want; they can also be petty or vindictive which is why I started with the fable of the scorpion and fox showing these characteristics.

Women can be friends but even then, they can be critical of each other of how they dress, act, and talk. Women have many different personalities which can conflict with each other. They can be friendly to your face and demeaning about you behind your back. Even those who are your friend can turn against you for the smallest slight and not explain what caused it.

Women meeting each other for the first time have been known to check each other out and see how they measure up to their standards. Even strangers check each other out. What if we wait to make a judgement and get to know them instead of judging quickly and completely without understanding or respect?   I like to watch people and ask questions. I have changed my opinion more than once when I made the effort to talk and ask questions about them and what they think. I am a very curious person and when I go anyplace, I give people a smile or even say hi as I go in the store or on the street. Other people I know with whom I have discussed this point, have done the same with the same result. Of course, we must make the effort.

What does it cost to give a smile or greeting? Nothing! Doing something nice for someone is also free. Just think, you might change your opinion. If not, at least you can accept them and maybe you were right in your first judgment. You don't have to love them but try respect and tolerance.

What is also insulting is that hurricanes and other violent storms were for many years named only for women. A single woman was called an old maid or a spinster while men were bachelors. Very obviously we were being looked upon as volatile, plain, and drab while men are the opposite.

There are also common phrases that we women use, and I have found myself using them. Do any sound familiar? Oh, go ahead, whatever, nothing, don't worry about it, I've got it, or fine and, of course, there is an inflection and tone along with saying it. And, last but not least, is the loud sigh.

And there are many women who are struggling just to survive that do not have the time. They are stressed and fearful trying to find the solutions to their problems. A smile goes a long way even to strangers. The list continues and yet women can also make you laugh and lift your spirits when you are depressed and even give you advice that helps you with a problem.   They mentor you and teach you things that they know, and you can have meaningful discussions about many subjects. You can also just have fun together!

Lucretia Mott, one of the original ladies of Seneca Falls had this to say about women, "The question is often asked, "What does woman want more than she enjoys? I answer, she wants to be acknowledged as a moral responsible being. She's seeking to be governed by laws in the making of which she has no voice. She is deprived of almost every right in civil society and is a cipher in the nation. Her duties marked by her equal brother man subject to creeds, rules and disciplines made for her by him is unworthy of her true dignity not cherished or protected as helpless children or adored angels man guide thinking and conduct." [5]

Women wanted independence and wanted to learn and were frustrated that they were not allowed to do so. Lucretia Mott also said once the suffrage movement started "The ideas of the leaders of this movement is not that women should be obliged to accept the privileges which we demand should be open to her. There are, no doubt, many women who have no inclination to mingle in the busy walks of life, and many would, in all probability, feel conscientious scruples against voting or taking any office under the present constitution of their country considering terms of its provisions. That, however, supplies no objection to the co-equality which we assert."[6]

---

[5] Lucretia Mott, Gentle Warrior, p. 155

Lucretia Mott

By the law that was common in this era, the husband and wife were considered one person and the husband was that person. What did that mean to women? Everything! No woman could speak in public, testify in court, preach from a pulpit, access equal education, control wages. She had no right of control over her children. If there was a divorce or separation, the woman had no right to custody of her children.

In 1819 there was a law that said a father could apprentice the children without the mother's permission or even put the children in apprenticeships to pay his debts. If her husband

---

[6] Library of Congress Social History Lucretia Mott

died, she had no right to any money; it went to a male heir either a son or other relative. Even a single woman had this problem. If a woman disobeyed her husband, she could be punished. In 1634 Maryland had a law on the books that said any woman inheriting money or property had to marry within seven years or lose it. She lost either way because once she married, her husband took control of all her assets.

You should clearly understand why women felt of little or less importance and wanted to make changes about their conditions. Women when together talked about their frustrations of being treated as inferior and having no rights to contribute in their own marriages. They talked as they were at church meetings or in their home, at suffrage, temperance, and abolitionist meetings and even personal conversations. The stories would be revealed of abuse, domination, and not being able to say or do anything. Most of the experiences related were all similar. Those same meetings taught them how to plan, organize, and put their beliefs into action which would become the foundation of their movement to petition, speak, and incite their beliefs to get other women to work for suffrage. Many women listened to the stories of others as to what they had endured.

One woman told how she and her children worked long and hard making butter and jam so there would be money to buy the children new clothes. When they earned enough to do this, the husband and father found out and confiscated all the money and went out and bought an expensive racehorse and paraded it down the streets of town.

One of the excuses often used by men and the anti-suffragists was that men or the husband's job was to take care of women. What father who loves his family would let them be dressed in rags? Because he could do what he wanted and had control over everything. What the children wore was his decision and wearing rags must have been fine with him. The mother in this case could do nothing and it devastated her and the children. It basically killed all hope for the mother, and she died in childbirth within a year. To quote Ernestine Rose "But it will be said that the husband provides for the wife, or in other words, he feeds, clothes, and shelters her! I wish I had the power to make everyone before me fully realize the degradation contained in that idea. Yes! He keeps her, and so he does a favorite horse, by law, they are both considered his property. . . Again I shall be told that the law presumes the husband to be kind, affectionate, and ready to provide and protect his wife. But what right, I   ask had the law to presume at all on the subject?   What right has the law to entrust the interest   and happiness of one being into the hands of another?" [7]

Another woman was married to a man and they took her money to pay his debts that he had incurred before they were married, and she was helpless to stop it. A third woman was married to a man and he decided to leave her but before he left town, he sold everything-the house, furniture and personal possessions including all her clothes. She was left with five young children and no means of support. People helped her get back on her feet finding her a place to live, furniture and even clothes. One man even gave her a loan to get her back on her feet. Unfortunately, the husband came back into town. He ignored the loan saying his wife had no right to conduct legal transactions which was true. He sold it all again and she was helpless and so were the others who had helped.

There were no laws to protect them; it was all in the hands of the husband or male. "Husband is entitled to wife's credit or business talents (whenever their intermarriage may have occurred); and goods purchased by her on her own credit, with his consent, while cohabiting with him, can be seized and sold in execution against him for his own debts, and this, though she carry on business in her

[7] Ladies of Seneca Falls, p. 12, Ernestine Rose

own name. . .There is nothing that an unruly wife might do against which the husband has not sufficient protection in the law. But not so the wife.[8] And how is the woman described? She is unruly going against the man's wishes thus being the inferior being.

In another example a deacon of a church would whip his wife in public every so often because she was cranky! This woman was the mother of six children for whom she cooked, cleaned, made their clothes besides helping with the farm and making butter, soap, and anything else that was needed to be done. He felt it necessary to remind her of her position. Again, she could not claim domestic abuse as there was no such law.

The Bible was used as proof that women were to be submissive to men and they quoted from the Bible. They used passages from the Bible that proclaim a lower status for women and girls. The Bible reference is Ephesians 5:22 "Wives submit yourselves unto your own husbands as unto the Lord. For the husband is the head of the wife." But in I Corinthians 7:3 it says, "Let the husband render unto the wife due benevolence; and likewise, also the wife unto the husband." There were women also in the Bible that were considered heroines for what they did for others and was not Mary the

---

[8] History of Woman Suffrage, p. v, p. 600

mother of Jesus?

What does the Bible say about women? Let's look at Genesis1: 26,27,31. "And God said, Let us make man in our image, after our likeness: and let them have dominion over the fish of the sea, and over the fowl of the air, and over the cattle, and over all the earth, and over every creeping thing that creepeth upon the earth. So, God created man in his own image, in the image of God created he him; male and <u>female</u> created he them. And God saw everything that he had made, and behold it was very good."

In Galatians 3:28 it also says, "There is neither male nor female; ye all one in Christ Jesus"

In Numbers 27: "the daughters of Zelophehad came before Moses and Eleazar saying our father has died with no male heir. Give unto us a portion a possession among the brethren of our father. Moses took unto the Lord and His answer "The daughters of Zelophehad speak right; thou shalt surely give them a possession of an inheritance among their father's brethren ;....And thou shalt speak unto the children of Israel saying If a man die and have no son then ye shall cause his inheritance to pass unto his daughter." The Bible thus supported women's rights, but these passages were ignored by the law and the clergy.

Instead Genesis 2 and other passages were used for their basis of argument. They called women the "daughters of Eve" for eating the apple and bringing evil and punishment for men. It was asserted that Eve was created from a rib of Adam and therefore inferior to the male and must suffer for her actions.

The clergy would become a nemesis for the suffrage movement using their interpretation of the Bible to defy giving equal rights to women. Women were considered cursed and the attitude and laws did not favor them. They were to be submissive and obedient. This is also basically the world attitude toward many women today. Men are superior and this is supported by passages from the Holy Bible and even other sacred texts that support physical punishment of women and girls and acceptance of violence to control them and keep them subordinate.

There will also be trouble from other sources including women who were anti-suffrage. But those who wanted suffrage and other rights did not let this impede them though they worked endlessly for their rights and being able to vote. There were many failures, but persistence and perseverance became their qualities to follow in their goal, but it took a long time!

Even women who were married had the problem of not having any money of their own since the husband controlled it all. He took care of the finances and paid all the bills. Women charged what they needed on an account which was then paid by the husband. This is where the practice of "charging a hat or coat" developed. The women would go to the seamstress or millinery store to order a new hat or coat. The lady doing the work would enter into an agreement with the wife to charge extra for the items. In return when the bill was paid, she would take a portion of the money and give the rest to the wife. It was devious but the only way the wife had money at her disposal.

The dissatisfaction and anger of the women and how they were curtailed by these laws developed into a need to find a way to solve the unfair and unequal treatment. As women began to talk to one another and see how others also had the same feelings that action began to take shape in protest with discussion, organization, and lots of work.

Their actions are what women who were seeking equal suffrage had to face in their long struggle from 1848 to 1920 and are still fighting inequality on many levels. That is a total of 72 years! Some of these women became the anti-suffragists who actively worked against the pioneers of suffrage. They were in good marriages where their husbands provided nice home and clothes and they did not understand how anybody else could complain about this! Except they had domestic help for the household chores and nannies that cared for the children as they dressed and went to luncheons and teas. The phrase the "woman's sphere" was often used. The home and motherhood were considered the first and last boundary of the woman.

But when the husband died, the wife was left to the mercy of the male heirs unless the husband had provided for the wife as the book Pride and Prejudice showed Darcy leaving 30,000 pounds to Elizabeth so she would not be penniless. If the husband did not do this, the widow was at the mercy of the heir. Even in this modern age, women have found wills that surprised them. One woman was married to a man for twenty years and when he died, he left absolutely nothing to her, so she was left homeless and lived on the streets. Or how about leaving money to another woman who had been his mistress or putting in clauses that tie the hands of the beneficiaries in selling property. Women should know what arrangements have been made and not leave it to a comment that everything will be fine; trust me, you are taken care of so don't worry about it. It is common sense to be aware of what has been provided in the will and other legal papers and most of all to know where to find the papers!

What is the world opinion of women and how did it and still does affect women? There are more women than men in the world, but men hold the dominant percentage of jobs except maybe in education where 75% of the teachers are women but only 20% of superintendents are women. There are mostly women in domestic service. Men also receive the highest salaries; women receive about 75 to 80% of what a man receives. In corporations, newscasting, actors in films, lawyers, judges, even in government jobs, in most cases the men receive higher wages. Higher paying jobs can be given to men by circumventing a title to indicate a man is doing more than a woman even though that probably is not the case; it's an excuse. In the last economic turndown, jobs that became available still went first to the men even in lower retail positions. Many women are head of households and the only source of money for that household.

What this means that throughout her life, a woman is earning only 3/4 of the money that a man does and therefore, her retirement is based on that lower amount which means a lower retirement. This puts women with a much lower income and single women account for about 40% of the households and with children. Their income is lower, and it usually means about half their income is spent on housing and it also means that companies do not offer them health services and other benefits. Lower salaries and benefits tend to put these women on the lower economic scale usually close to or below poverty. At retirement it also usually means there are twice as many women in poverty as men.

As women were told from the beginning that they were inferior and the weaker sex in every way, it is a belief that carries through to this day and is passed from generation to generation. Even as girls attended school and got an education, they did not go into mathematics or the sciences as they were told they were unable to comprehend or understand these subjects and boys would not be interested in them or consider them attractive. They were incompetent of being engineers, computer analysts, doctors, or research scientists yet this has been proved false as women go into these fields and succeed.

Narcissa Whitman and Eliza Spaulding were the first white women to go west of the Mississippi River heading to Oregon. As they traveled over the land, Narcissa explored the rock and plants, collected them, drew pictures, and wrote about them in detail. How was it possible for her to do all this when she was considered inept and unable to understand what she was doing? They both helped build new homes in the west and worked hard and helped their neighbors even nursing them and were missionaries in this new area.

We have a good supply of future scientists; we don't need to bring them in from foreign countries only train and educate more and more women and encourage them to go into these math and science fields.

How about Mary Jackson, Katherine Johnson, and Dorothy Vaughn? They were African Americans who worked for NASA (National Aeronautics and Space Administration) as engineers and mathematicians in the 1950's and 1960's in Langley, Virginia. There was still segregation at that time until the late 1950's.

Katherine Johnson was a prodigy graduating from college at the age of eighteen. She was the first black female at West Virginia State. She was originally a teacher but heard NASA was hiring African women. Her first job was to study the black boxes of airplanes that had crashed. What she discovered from a black box of a small plane that had fallen out of the sky without warning was that larger planes had the ability to disturb the air space when flying through it for at least a half-hour after the flight. This caused the smaller plane to be flipped and lose control.

Katherine's main job was to calculate the trajectories which allowed astronauts to return home from the moon. When Alan Shephard was an astronaut and asked her to check figures, she would plot the course for him. John Glenn also asked her to check the figures of the computer and if she agreed, then the mission was a go. He said he trusted her more than the computer.

Mary Jackson was a mathematician and aerospace engineer starting in 1958 at Langley Research. Dorothy Vaughn was also a mathematician or human computer at Langley. In 1949, she was appointed acting supervisor, the only African American, and prepared for the introduction of computers. She taught herself the programming language the very proof that women were equally capable of learning math and sciences and doing well in those jobs.

The next problem is sexual harassment, rape and particularly sex trafficking. Many girls beginning at an early age and through middle age are harassed by men who are sexual predators. Girls in the middle school are harassed at school, by texting, or on the internet.

It is estimated that one in five college girls are raped but they do not report it and military women are also raped. If they report the incident, they are recommended to drop it and if not, they face retaliation. Domestic violence accounts for 75% of injury to women from age 18 to around 45.

`The worst travesty is sex trafficking where an estimated 25 million women and men are abducted, enticed, and manipulated to meet people who will then use them as a business to sell outright or use as prostitutes. These women are runaways or minorities but also from middle class families. Girls are enticed through the internet by their predators who promises each girl things; they are also kidnapped and used for the same purpose. When they agree to meet them, they are seized and become their property. They are basically enslaved and forced to carry out business deals. If they try to escape, they are found and punished or even killed.

The three biggest countries that make the most from this business are the United States, Mexico, and the Philippines. The dollar amount of this business is estimated to be around 35 billion dollars. These girls are NOT all shipped to other countries; they stay HERE. In this country where we have a Constitution, women are bought and sold! A man who recently committed suicide or was killed was noted for being in the sex trafficking business. Are the children coming into the U.S. illegally being exploited for this reason?

So, we will begin the story as a result of my search for answers about the length of time to get suffrage and about the women involved. I realized I needed the background of the women and what these women had done before their commitment to suffrage. Where did these women fit in the history of suffrage and what did they contribute? To do this I researched their backgrounds and the timeframe in which they worked. As I found one to include, someone else emerged as part of the story. I also wanted to condense the enormous amount of material into a more concise history so that you would learn about the women as you read the history. There are numerous sources to find information-the library has numerous books, The Library of Congress has a much bigger archive of historical documents, and of course, you can google. The 19th amendment was the most disputed in the history of the U.S and took the most time. During the American Revolution and Civil War and even World War I, who took over the work men had done while they went to fight? The answer is women did it all.

I sought for answers just as others have done including the well-known aviator Amelia Earhart. Amelia Earhart wrote this in a note to her husband when she started off on her ill-fated flight around the world in 1937, "Please know that I am quite aware of the hazards. I want to do it because I want to do it. Women must try to do things as men have tried.

When they fail, their failure must be but a challenge to others."[9]   I also wanted to do it to see if I could find the answers.

---

[9] Notes before last flight in 1937 by George Putnam of Amelia Earhart, p. 9

EARLY PIONEERS OF SUFFRAGE

Charging a Hat or Coat

The first women in my story are those who were not in the suffrage movement but were suffragists by forging their own goals and beliefs even with opposition from others. They dared to pursue their goals and pushed the boundaries of what was expected.

They proved that women were intelligent and knew how to articulate their philosophies to the public even against the opposition and ridicule. Many women were also forced to work when their husbands left for war, deserted them, or died; they were left having to support the family.

Mary Wollstonecraft, Lucretia Mott, and Elizabeth Cady Stanton all stressed education as one of the vital points of improving the lives of women. From the early pioneers of suffrage, you will read again and again how they worked to get an education, most of them earning their own way.

We know of Seneca Falls and the beginning of the struggle to gain voting and other rights for women but why did it take till 1920 to achieve that goal? I am going to write this story as close to chronological history as possible and tell you their background as you read. You can research more as you wish. Maybe it will inspire you to research women in your family who possibly were involved in this period and there is still much to find out. There is still not total equality and more work needs to be done.

Margaret Brent was born in Gloucester, England in 1601. She was one of thirteen children in a Catholic family. Catholics were persecuted there, and the family decided to come to America to the colony of Maryland which had been started as a safe haven for Catholics by George Calvert known as Lord Baltimore. She bought land and managed the property having watched her father at home. The year was 1638. They built houses and brought settlers to this new land. She became a large landowner. She also became the executor of Lord Calvert's property after he passed away.

In 1648, she demanded her right to vote in the House of Burgesses because owning land was a qualification. Here was an early woman who demanded the right to vote when women were a nonentity.

They refused to allow her the right to vote yet they made her pay taxes. This was before the time of the American Revolution, yet she still opposed being taxed without being allowed representation. She then sold both pieces of property and used the money to pay soldiers who had helped defend the colony and had not been paid for their services. The rest of the money she used to leave Maryland and go elsewhere.

She then went to settle in Virginia where she bought land and managed it. Some women could vote in early days in New York, New Jersey, Massachusetts, New Hampshire but the new country took those rights away when the Constitution was written and approved, although New Jersey had it after till 1807. She had attempted to vote in 1648 and was denied. Two hundred years later in 1848, the Seneca Falls convention commenced to start the movement.

Fanny Wright came over with Lafayette during the American Revolution in the1770's and bought land. She proceeded to teach slaves to read and write and was the first woman to speak in public about slavery and women's rights.

These women overcame prejudices and attempted to achieve what they wanted done. It is hard to uncover what many women did in the early years because there were no books written about their exploits. Their personal diaries and journals are the best source we have and thankfully, their families preserved these historical facts. What information we do have comes from people writing in a diary or journal about their lives.

Elizabeth Whitman is a good example. She had told her family to destroy her journals after her death. She also wrote many letters to her family telling them about her life and experiences. Thank goodness, they ignored the request. In the writings that we do have from women, they all stressed education as the leading factor. There were and are hundreds of such women. They were pioneers in fields that women had never entered, and they made a name for themselves.

Biddy Mason was a former slave born August 15, 1818 in Hancock, Georgia at times living in Georgia, Mississippi, and South Carolina. She was given as a wedding present to Robert Smith and his wife. Smith took her to Mississippi and then Nauvoo, Illinois, one of the centers of the Mormon religion. From there they joined the Mormons for the trek to Salt Lake City, Utah, the head of the Mormon church which still is today. They had already given suffrage to women.

Robert Smith was sent to California by Brigham Young who told him to free his slaves before he moved to California. While there, Biddy sued for her freedom in 1856 having lived in Utah which was a free state. She included all the other slaves there. It was a bold and courageous move for her to have made at that time. In 1860 all received the documentation of their freedom. She achieved freedom before the Civil War had even started!

Biddy began working as a nurse and midwife. She was very frugal with her money being able to save well. She then proceeded to buy land and when it increased in value, she bought more and more until she was very comfortable having a net worth of over $300,000 which at that point in time was high. She used her money to help the poor opening a daycare center where children could come. She donated land for the African Methodist Episcopal Church in Los Angeles. She was well known around town like with the Pio Rico Governor of Alta California and eventually lived with Robert Owens, another wealthy businessman and his son who ended up married to one of her daughters. She died January 15, 1891 and was buried in an unmarked grave but on March 27, 1988 a marker was placed at her gravesite in Georgia.

Another woman who was a contemporary of Elizabeth Cady Stanton and Susan B. Anthony was Mary Baker Eddy. She was the founder of the First Church of Christ, Scientist and author of the book Science and Health published in 1875.

Mary Baker Eddy

She was born July 16, 1821 in Bow, New Hampshire. As a young child, she was often ill but seemed to grow out of it. She studied the Bible her whole life and was healed in 1866 from a fall by reading the Bible.

She was married in 1843 to George Washington Glover, a friend of her brother, Samuel, and moved to South Carolina. Unfortunately, he passed away six months later, and she moved back home pregnant with her first child. After her son was born, she was quite ill and not able to take care of him. Her son, George, was sent with relatives out west. Because she was weak and had little money, she lost custody. She attempted several times to regain custody but failed in her efforts so that is where he grew up; they met in later years, but their lives had taken different courses and they were not close.

In 1866 during the winter, Mary took a bad fall on the ice and was brought back to her apartment and a doctor was called. She was not really expected to live. She asked friends to bring her Bible which had been a common practice throughout her life. By reading it, she was healed. After her healing, she dedicated her life writing about the experience trying to find the answer to her healing. It took three years for the writing of her book. The rest of her life was dedicated in starting her religion and setting up its organization.

Mary Baker Eddy used her own name and not a pseudonym as other women had to do. She was not in the suffrage movement but proved she could achieve her goal. She conducted business under her own name. She earned and kept her own money when women held the lowest paying jobs and were subservient to men. She spoke in public and gave lectures when women were denied that right. She was the founder and president of a teaching college when women were denied the right to get an education and kept out in most cases. She made front page news when women's history was suppressed. She built and conducted her own church.

She passed away in 1910 leaving the church well organized and operating.

In 1998 she was inducted into the Women's Hall of Fame as one of the top 25 most influential religious figures of the 20th century. In 1999 the National Foundation of Women Legislators recognized her contribution to journalism and in 2000 she was recognized in - Extraordinary Women who changed History as one of the leading female religious figures of modern times. She was not a member of the suffrage movement but knew what was occurring as she wrote. She was also well acquainted with Mark Twain and even though he disagreed with her views, he had great respect for her achievements. She was too busy building her church, teaching, organizing and leading her church.

Helen Stewart was born April 16, 1854 in Springfield, Illinois. Her maiden name was Helen Jane Wiser. Her family moved to Iowa when she was nine and then to California. The family moved to Galt, California to a two-story house which originally came from the east and had been taken apart brought around the Horn of South America and reconstructed in California. Helen went to school in Sacramento County and attended at least one year of college at Hesperian College in Woodland.

Archibald Stewart became her husband on April 6, 1873 in Stockton, California. He had been born in Ireland but of Scottish descent. He owned and operated a freighting business in Pioche, Nevada. Three of her children were born there- William James, Hiram Richard, and Flora Elizabeth, known as Tiza, her whole life.

Archibald loaned $5,000 to Octavius Gass, who used his ranch as collateral. Two years later he defaulted on the loan and the family moved to the ranch to farm and use it as a way station. Here Evaline La Vega was born. Helen was a busy woman but managed to become friends with the Paiute Indian women and kept records of their basket making and the stories that they told. She accumulated 550 of them and left them to the state of Nevada.

One day in 1884 Helen received a note from a neighbor, Conrad Kiel, telling her to bring a wagon and pick up the body of her husband who had been murdered. Leaving her four young children and pregnant with her fifth, she rushed over there to see what had happened to her husband and found him dead having numerous wounds with no explanation of what had happened. She transferred him back home and in order to have a coffin, she requested that the farm hands take off the doors of the house to construct a coffin.

The men who had killed him were not arrested or one of them was and put in jail. There were no eyewitnesses only Helen Stewart and the men Conrad Keil and Hank Parrish. They were not indicted and there was no punishment or justice. Parrish would be hanged for other misdeeds which when Helen found out, she recorded the event in her diary and underlined the passage. Archibald's death was never solved.

Helen had no experience with ranching but was forced into it; she could ranch or sell the land. By her lawyer's advice she went to the county board asking for a widow's tax exemption of $1,000 which they gave her but in the same meeting raised her taxes $1,000. Archibald had been a good businessman but not well liked; there was no law to protect her interests and a woman with no rights had no way to repudiate the law.

Helen went back to her parents in Galt to have her fifth child, Archie, named after her deceased husband, Archibald, while her father came to the ranch to run it for her. Coming back to the ranch after Archie's birth, she attempted to try and sell it with no luck, so she learned to run it and became very proficient. She kept buying up land close to her so that by 1890, she was the largest landowner around there; she owned over 2,000 acres growing vegetables and raising cattle to sell meat to the miners and other people living there. They also appointed her the first postmaster in 1893 in Las Vegas where she served till 1903. Again, here is a woman who ran a ranch successfully and was a postmistress when women were considered lacking knowledge and capability to handle such responsibilities.

Concerned that her children were not getting an adequate education in the isolated area where her ranch was located, she hired a tutor and sent three children to a boarding school. Because she felt they needed more, Helen Stewart sold the ranch in 1902 to the San Pedro Los Angeles and Salt Lake Railroad. Her youngest son, Archie, had been killed at the ranch chasing wild horses.

The family moved to L.A. and built a new house. One room of the original house is now in the L.A. museum. Stewart married Frank Stewart who had worked many years on the ranch. She did not take his name but remained Helen Stewart. Frank also had to sign a prenuptial to the effect that all her money and belongings would go to her children. That was a great achievement for a woman when women had few rights. At the same time, she lost another son, Hiram, who had two children.

In Los Angeles Helen enjoyed a social life and founded the Christ Episcopal Church and the Mesquite Club.   In the historical society that she started, she urged women to record stories of their lives leaving a history of their life and achievements She died March 6, 1926. Her obituary only listed her as a historian not as a rancher or a woman who ran a thriving business giving her no credit for that success. Obviously, there was a great deal of prejudice. History, though, gave Helen Stewart the title "The first lady of Las Vegas".

Justina Ford was born January 22,1871 in Knoxville, Illinois one of seven children. Her parents were Pryor and Melissa both former slaves. Her father died when she was seven.

Her mother was a nurse and when she visited her patients, Justina went with her to observe and help. Justina wanted to be a doctor from the time she was a young child always playing the part of the doctor with her friends and siblings making up names for various diseases. She even dissected frogs for practice. The suffrage movement had been in operation since 1848; her goal was to be a doctor not a suffragist. She would face prejudice on two issues being African American and a woman.

Justina Ford

After graduating from Galesburg High School, an integrated school, Justina attended Herring Medical College in Chicago getting degrees in gynecology, obstetrics, and pediatrics in 1899. While there she met and married John Ford and they lived in Chicago and then moved to Alabama. They faced too much prejudice there and relocated to Colorado where she applied for a medical license.

She took the test and passed even though the person giving the test apologized about taking her money because she would not be allowed to practice first being a woman and second being an African American. She was determined to be a doctor but was not allowed hospital privileges till late in her career.

She was Denver's first licensed female African American doctor. She accepted all patients regardless of race, color, gender, language, or ability to pay. She had her practice in her home or she was driven to them. She knew multiple languages which helped her to communicate to her patients. Many of them paid her in goods or services.

She divorced John Ford in 1912 and married Alfred Allen who would drive her to house calls. Late in her life was she even allowed hospital privileges; all her deliveries were at home. She delivered over 7,000 babies in her life. After all the years of not having hospital privileges, Justina joined the Colorado Medical Society in 1950. She was also awarded the Human Rights Award from Denver's Cosmopolitan Club. She died October 14, 1952 and worked till her death.

Julia Morgan was the first licensed architect in California; she designed over 700 buildings, but a lot of people did not know her as she avoided publicity. The information that there is about her came from family members who had her papers; there were no books in the library about her achievements. She was born on January 22, 1872 (same age as Justina Ford) in San Francisco coming from a wealthy family. Her father had come around South America to reach California. There was no Panama Canal to shorten the journey. In California he made his money.

Julia was one of five siblings. She never married devoting herself to her career. She went to the University of California studying civil engineering as they did not have a program for architecture. In her senior year, she had a professor by the name of Bernard Maybeck. He gave her advice to study in Paris by entering a competition for architects; the school was the Ecole de Beau Arts in Paris. They were dubious about letting an American into the college even though they had lifted a ban not allowing women. Maybeck persuaded her to keep trying as the Beau Arts in France was considered the best architectural school at that time; she was twenty-six. She achieved her architect's license in 1904, the first woman to do so. She and Maybeck remained friends for the rest of their lives.

Phoebe Hearst was funding the competition and had offered to pay her expenses, but Julia refused and earned her own way. Julia completed the requirements in one year and was granted a certificate. She returned to the United States and began working for John Galen Howard, a prominent West Coast architect who was director of the

University of California building program at Mills College.

Phoebe Hearst once again met her and used her influence to get her the job; Phoebe was very much involved in suffrage work. She would become a member of the NWP (National Working Party) with Alice Paul as the leader.   Mr. Howard proceeded to give her the responsibility of the job. Julia was responsible for this work including the Tower Hall. Mrs. Hearst admired her work so much she was given the responsibility of the theater project. But she left the firm in 1905 when she heard the comment that Mr. Howard had said he possessed the best and most talented designer, whom I have to pay almost nothing, as it is a woman.

What was she supposed to do about that? Could she sue him for sexual discrimination? Were there government laws that protected her from pay inequalities? The answer to both is no! She was a woman. But she did not give up! Julia Morgan left the employ of Mr. Howard and opened her own architectural office. Because her creditability was noted, she was given commissions. Phoebe Hearst was a well-known philanthropist and a worker in the suffrage movement. Although I do not believe Julia was active in it, she received jobs from the network of suffrage workers. Phoebe Hearst recommended her for jobs even to her son, William Randolph Hearst.

Buildings by Julia Morgan included El Campanile at Mills College, and Asilomar, the YWCA building, which was made a state park in 1956. San Simeon is also a state park now but was built by Julia; it took years for her to finish the project from 1919 to 1947; it was composed of 143 rooms filled with items that William Randolph Hearst had collected; it was made a state park in 1958 and both of these places are desirable and profitable visiting sites.

When the earthquake of 1906 destroyed much of San Francisco, Julia was chosen as the architect for rebuilding. It had come to the notice of developers that Tower Hall on the Mills campus had remained intact from the earthquake because of Julia's design which was to use reinforced granite inside the tower which kept the tower from disintegrating. The Fairmont hotel was given to her to rebuild; all that had been left was the shell from the earthquake, so the builders awarded her the commission. A woman architect designed and built structures able to withstand earthquakes when male architects had not achieved such results.

Julia was considered an excellent designer and trained her employees the same way. She demanded the best and worked hard expecting her employees to do the same sometimes seven days a week. Her employees who worked with her were well trained and got other jobs quickly because of their training. Julia Morgan did not receive recognition at her death for her achievements as with the other women I have discussed. In 2014, years after her death in 1957, she was posthumously given the American Institute of Architects Gold Medal, again a first for a woman.

You would think the story of Julia Morgan would have set a precedent for women. They had achieved the right to vote in 1920 but not enough other rights that there was not discrimination against women. The next lady was much later but faced sex discrimination on her job.

Lily Ledbetter was working for Goodyear Tire and Rubber Company. She started in 1979 working as a shift manager. She had two children and her husband was in the military. Soon after she was hired, she was asked to sign a contract policy that barred her from asking about contract rates. She worked there many years and was given the Top Performance in 1996 but had gotten low performance ratings before that which diminished her pay increases. In 1998 she had come into work early and an anonymous note had been dropped in her mailbox showing her pay rate of $3,727 a month and fifteen male workers with salaries of $4,286 to

$5,236. That meant that her pay was from $500.- $1,500 less a month than the others. Add that up and see the difference in retirement between her and the men! And it was a very good reason for women to fight for their rights against such treatment.

She sued Goodyear in an equal pay lawsuit based on sex discrimination to fight this inequality and the case was brought before the Equal Employment Commission.

She won in the first trial and was given back pay and punitive damages in the amount of $36,000 but Goodyear appealed it. In the court of appeals, she lost the case and it went to the Supreme Court. The case first opened on November 27, 2006 and the decision read on May 29, 2007. They decreed that it had been too long by the terms of the Civil Rights Act of 1964 that it could be no more than 180 days from the disparity of pay and the law; in fact, it had been somewhere around 20 years where she had been underpaid. Title VII had allowed companies to still discriminate on gender employees. It would take a law of Congress to change it The Supreme Court decision was 5 to 4. A dissenting opinion by Ruth Bader Ginsburg, along with Justices Breyer, Souter, and Stevens said the defendants should seek to have Congress review the law and pass a new law correcting the problem.

In 2009 the Lily Ledbetter Fair Pay Act was passed and signed when the 1964 Civil Rights Act was amended along with the Equal Pay Act.

One of the women responsible for getting the Civil Rights Act of 1964 passed was Alice Paul, a suffragette who also helped get the 19th amendment added to the Constitution. She was still alive in 1964. You will read about her further on in the book.

All the previous women mentioned were seeking equality in their lives. They wanted careers of their own choosing even though society refused them the right just by the nature of their gender. They achieved their goals and proved to all women that it was possible if they had the determination. There were many other women who achieved similar goals of which we have no written proof of their efforts, but they should all be celebrated for their fortitude. Now let's begin the long journey of organized suffrage.

THE BEGINNING OF THE SUFFRAGIST MOVEMENT

Charging a Hat or Coat

In the 1800's jobs available to women included running a boarding house, doing laundry, sewing clothes, and making hats, running a dry goods store or millenary, and being a teacher at a reduced pay.

In the 1880's women could be nurses, day laborers, maids, housekeepers, and teachers at a reduced pay. By 1917, women could become secretaries because men had gone off to fight in W.W. I. Being a secretary, has in modern times only been considered a woman's job but the fact was only men were secretaries until World War I.

In the 1960's women were nurses, librarians, secretaries, teachers, who were not recommended to go into the sciences, housekeepers, waitresses, maids and other menial jobs.

In 1848 in Seneca Falls, New York, five women gathered for what is now known as the beginning of the Women' s Rights Movement. Four of the women were Quakers-Lucretia Mott of Philadelphia, her sister, Martha Wright, Jane Hunt, and Mary Ann McClintock. Elizabeth Cady Stanton who was the wife of an abolitionist Henry Stanton, was the fifth person. She was discontented in her role of wife and a woman who had few rights or voice in what was happening. It was a very common role for women. She had met Lucretia Mott at a World Anti-Slavery meeting in London in 1840. Even though Lucretia was a delegate to the convention, they would not allow her to speak because she was a woman; she had to sit in the balcony and that is where she met Elizabeth Cady Stanton. As Elizabeth was also sitting there in the balcony, the two women became acquainted and discussed their viewpoints and goals for women and themselves.

But the most organized effort to get the vote for women began in 1848 at the Seneca Falls Convention. Almost every woman involved in women's rights had also been active in the temperance movement and the abolition of slavery. These were the three most important reform movements in the 19th century. This work taught them how to speak, to organize, to hold public meetings, and to conduct petition campaigns and how to handle criticism and jeering from men.

The year 1848 was marked by revolutions and reforms both in Europe and in the United States. Dorothea Dix had worked alone for ten years trying to get better treatment in mental hospitals. In 1848, one such bill passed Congress, but the president vetoed it. People were trying to change things for the better.

It was also the year gold was discovered in California which caused a massive drive of settlers rushing to get to the west to find gold. Europeans also came to the United States seeking a new way of life and freedom. These immigrants came here legally usually through New York and were processed and given medical exams and their names and background recorded. It did not mean they became citizens but were able to get land and jobs. The West was an open arena for new ideas and beginnings; the boundaries of the United States were almost complete. In this climate the seeds of reform came into bloom for the women's rights movement.

There was change coming slowly. Lucy Stone had graduated from Oberlin College in 1847 being the first woman to do so. Elizabeth Cady Stanton had been working for married women's property rights in New York and got it passed in 1848. Unfortunately, New York repealed it in 1862. Now married women could control and sell their property without the husband's permission. They also could inherit money. They also could have guardianship of their children if there was separation or a divorce. It appealed to wealthy Dutch landowners too who wanted to protect their holdings from the hands of their sons-in-laws from gambling or squandering the bank accounts.

Anesthesia had been developed for use with patients but when it was attempted to be used with the birth process, the clergy loudly protested saying it was against the Bible. It says in Genesis 3: 16, "in sorrow thou shalt bring forth children; and thy desire shall be to thy husband, and he shall rule over thee". What an awful condemnation to put on women and another mark against the humanity of women.

In 1848 there was no state where you could legally speak in public, testify in court, preach from the pulpit, have access to equal education, control your own wages and property, except New York for a while, or enter other professions. In 1900 not one state denied all of these.   Forty thousand women were enrolled in colleges and there were already 30,000 alumnae. The A.A.U.W. (American Association of Women) was started in 1881 in Boston, Massachusetts) dedicated to promoting. "education and equity for all women and girls" Three million women were working in professions other than domestic service. In 2/3 of the states, the women owned their own wages, and 3/4 of the states allowed women to own property separate from their husband. But only four states-Wyoming, Utah, Colorado, and Idaho had granted full suffrage. So here the struggle begins in Seneca, New York.

Elizabeth Cady Stanton and Lucretia Mott had already met in 1840 at the London Antislavery meeting. They became very friendly and discussed women's rights as they were there which included the books of Mary Wollstonecraft and Margaret Fuller. They agreed to keep in contact. Elizabeth Stanton had this to say about her meeting with Lucretia Mott. "When I first heard from the lips of Lucretia Mott. . .that I had the same right to think for myself that Martin Luther, John Calvin, and John Knox had and the same right to be guided by my own convictions, and would no doubt live . . .a happier life than if guided by theirs, I felt at once a new-born sense of dignity and freedom."[10] These women she met believed in the equality of the sexes.

In 1848, Lucretia contacted Elizabeth Stanton with the intent of having a meeting about women's rights. The women met at the home of Jane and Richard Hunt in Waterloo, New York to organize a meeting. The meeting was held at a mahogany

---

[10] Ladies of Seneca Falls, p. 84

table in their home where they wrote their "Declaration of Rights".

On July 19 and 20 1848, in Seneca Falls, New York the first woman's rights convention was held where Elizabeth Cady Stanton lived. They decided to put an ad in the newspaper to see if anyone would come. The ad ran eight days before the scheduled meeting.

Elizabeth Cady Stanton   **Lucretia Mott**

It read "WOMAN'S RIGHTS CONVENTION A convention to discuss the social, civil, and religious conditions and rights of women, will be held in the Wesleyan Chapel, at Seneca Falls, N.Y., on Wednesday and Thursday the 19th and 20th of July, current; commencing at 10:00 A.M. During the first day the meeting will be exclusively for women, who are earnestly invited to attend. The public generally are invited to be present the second day, when Lucretia Mott, of Philadelphia, and other ladies and gentlemen, will address the convention."[11]

It was held in the Wesleyan chapel built by the congregation. It was thought large enough to hold a larger group.   Mary McClintock, Martha Wright (sister of Lucretia Mott} and Jane Hunt were the other organizers of this convention. Carriages and wagon loads formed a procession to Wesleyan Hall along with those who were walking from the local area.

Mary McClintock

Martha Wright

Jane Hunt

---

[11] Gentle Warrior, p. 156, History of Woman Suffrage, v. 1, p. 67

About forty men came to the meeting including men like William Lloyd Garrison, a prominent abolitionist, journalist, and social reformer who would become a suffragist too. Frederick Douglass, the only African American and editor of the newspaper, **The North Star,** would also work as an abolitionist and supported suffrage. He was thirty-one now and had escaped from slavery when he was twenty-one. There were estimated to be 300 people at this first meeting.

Only women were supposed to talk the first day; James Mott was the chairman of the convention since women could not do this.   The other man at the meeting was Thomas McClintock, husband of Mary Jane. The first speaker was Lucretia Mott, wife of James; she was very comfortable with speaking as she was a Quaker and used to speaking in church. Her main point was that education was the key to changing the status of women. Quakers believed in equality of men and women. They were able to participate and speak in the church service. The Quakers were the first to work against slavery by boycotting goods that had been created or picked by any slave labor.

Elizabeth Cady Stanton, the second speaker had never spoken before but managed to deliver her speech and even enjoyed it even being so nervous. She would become a popular speaker and writer.   Elizabeth had written the Declaration of Sentiments at the round mahogany table in the home of Mary McClintock which now resides in the Smithsonian Institution in Washington, D.C. but had also been given to Susan B. Anthony and was in her home in Rochester, New York when she retired.

Elizabeth had help from her husband, Henry, who was a lawyer and helped with describing all the barriers women faced. He agreed with all of them except the ninth which was the right of suffrage. He said it should not be in there and to show his anger when Elizabeth refused to remove it, left town in protest. He was running for political office and felt this would hinder him in the election.

There were thirteen resolutions presented called the Declaration of Rights; it was patterned after the Declaration of Independence. A quote from The Declaration of Sentiments introduces their philosophy, "The history of mankind is a history of repeated injuries and usurpations on the part of men toward women having in direct object the establishment of an absolute tyranny over her. To prove this let facts be submitted to a candid world. He has never permitted her to exercise her inalienable right to the elective franchise. He has compelled her to submit to laws, in the formation of which she had no voice. He has withheld from her rights which are given to the most ignorant and degraded men…He has made her, if married in the eyes of the law, civilly dead."[12] The rights listed to men should also be included for women and the rights demanded by men also extended to women. The Declaration of Independence gave its resolutions which so did the women in the Declaration of Rights. All resolutions were discussed even having the right of divorce with incompatibility as a cause but that was not accepted and the one that took the longest was the right of elective franchise giving women the right to vote.

Many women were shocked at the idea and refused this point as being too radical, but it still passed by a narrow margin. Even Lucretia was very reticent about the right of women being able to vote as even Quaker women did not vote in their churches. Yet Lucretia supported Elizabeth Stanton in the elective franchise even though it was against her personal belief and voted for it. This was what women should do for each other and Lucretia did. The rights women had been denied included rights of citizens and representation. "Resolved, That all laws which prevent women from occupying such a station in society as her conscience shall dictate, or which place her in a position inferior to that of man, are contrary to the great precept of nature, and therefore of no force or authority. Resolved That

---

[12] History of Woman Suffrage, v. 1 , p. 70

woman is man's equal-was intended to be so by the Creator, demands that she should be recognized as such. Resolved That it is the duty of the women of this country to secure to themselves the sacred right of elective franchise."[13]   All resolutions were approved by the women at Seneca Falls even the elective franchise.

There were 100 people that signed the Declaration of Rights and thirty- two of them were men. The women expected and received condemnation and criticism from the public but kept moving forward with suffrage. The bad press given them actually helped in that people read of their actions and learned what was happening. They knew they would keep meeting, working, and giving speeches wherever they were allowed.

The newspapers that wrote about the convention called it a joke.   They gave names to it like "The Reign of Petticoats", "Bolting Among the Ladies", "Petticoats versus Boots" and "Insurrection Among Women". The only fair reporter from the *Tribune* was Horace Greeley. He became a supporter of suffrage and articles written by Elizabeth Stanton were printed in the newspaper. Margaret Fuller had once been a writer for the newspaper, was well educated and respected by

---

[13] History of Woman Suffrage, v. 1, p. 71

Horace Greeley. So, he was agreeable about printing the events at Seneca Falls.

At this first meeting was a nineteen-year old schoolteacher named Charlotte Woodward who also did piecework for a glove factory in Seneca. She was a Quaker and was one of the women who had traveled the farthest to attend the convention. She came in a wagon with farm horses. She had read the notice in the paper and had gone to her neighbors asking them to go also. Her fellow workers also came to the meeting as the people in the factories realized how exploited they were at work as they were paid less and worked longer than men. She and her friends came in a carriage and said at the beginning of the trip, they were the only ones on the road but when they came to a crossroads, they encountered other carriages with women.

This happened again and again; soon there was long procession of women all going to Wesleyan Hall. Her words about the convention: "I do not believe there any community anywhere in which the soul of some women was not beating their wings in rebellion. Every fiber of my being rebelled although silently all the hours that I sat and sewed gloves for a miserable pittance, which after it was earned could never be mine. I wanted to work, but I wanted to choose my task and I wanted to collect my wages." [14] She signed the declaration and will be the only woman at Seneca Falls who will be still alive to vote in 1920; she was 92 years old and very ill.

This was the first Woman's Rights convention; the second one was two weeks later at the Unitarian Church in Rochester, New York. Because of the horrendous publicity about the first convention, the women were nervous about a second meeting even Elizabeth Stanton, but she still agreed to help with the second with "fear and trembling". What they had been brainwashed with growing up about being inferior came back to haunt them. It was Lucretia Mott that persuaded them they were heading in the right direction saying to the effect that education was the answer to being inferior and knowing about the world around them. It must have been very daunting to these women realizing that they had embarked on a journey that no one else had dared. They kept true to their commitment and followed it to the end.

Lucretia Mott said, "We deny that the present position of women is her true sphere of usefulness; nor will she attain to this sphere, until the disabilities and disadvantages, religious, civil, and social, which

[14] National Historical Park Service, Interview by Rheta Childe Dorr of Charlotte Woodward

impede her progress, are removed out of her way. These restrictions have enervated her mind and paralyzed her powers. While man assumes that the present is the original state designed for women, that the existing differences are not arbitrary. . .but grounded in nature, she will not make the necessary effort to obtain her just rights, lest it should subject her to the kind of scorn and contemptuous manner in which she has been spoken of." [15] The women's sphere was claimed only to be at home.

The second convention was organized by three women Amy Post, Rhoda Degarmo, and Sarah Fish. They met and organized and chose Abigail Bush as the president of the meeting; the meeting was August 2, 1848. Elizabeth Stanton and Lucretia Mott were solidly against this thinking as they were the honored guests invited to the meeting. They felt a woman did not have the experience of rules and order which is why James Mott had chaired the Seneca Falls meeting.

The three organizers urged Stanton and Mott to reconsider and the two left the podium and sat in the audience. Even though Elizabeth Cady Stanton and Lucretia Mott both protested this action, they let the presider take over the meeting and they sat in the audience. The convention was only one day, and Abigail Bush chaired all three sessions.

---

[15] Ladies of Seneca Falls, p. 47

Stanton and Mott apologized to Bush and admitted what a good job she had done. There were even more people at this meeting. At the second meeting, the right of suffrage was included as part of the Declaration of Rights with even more people voting for it.

Elizabeth Cady Stanton   **Lucretia Mott**

Four conventions were held in in 1850 in Ohio beginning in Salem. The first National Women's Convention was held in Worcester, New York October 1850 and every year after that, except in 1857, until the Civil War. After the war, they started again and this time the conventions were organized and held each year till the 19th Amendment was passed. The national convention and other meetings would remain the main source of communication for women till after the Civil War. They would remain the grassroots of women for organizing and learning how to conduct meetings.

There were also regional meetings in Syracuse, New York, Cleveland, Ohio, Philadelphia, Pennsylvania, Cincinnati, Ohio, and New York, New York, Pennsylvania, Ohio, and others as the movement grew in size and influence.

Seneca Falls was a small meeting in a small town. What brought the most publicity were the newspapers that belittled the women and expressed outrage that the women dared to demand equal rights. This was mainly a white upper- class event and even women who were well provided by their husbands were intrigued with what was being written in the newspapers. It appealed to their sensibilities for reform to work in this movement.

Frederick Douglass

On July 25, after Seneca Falls, Frederick Douglass published in his newspaper, **the North Star**, an editorial about the convention that had just been held.

"One of the most interesting events of the past week, was the holding of what is technically styled a Woman's Rights Convention at Seneca Falls. The speaking, addresses, and resolutions of this extraordinary meeting were almost wholly conducted by women, and although they evidently felt themselves in a novel position, it is but simple justice to say that their whole proceedings were characterized by marked ability and dignity.

Many who have at last made the discovery that the negroes have some rights as well as others of the human family, have yet to be convinced that women are entitled to any. Eight years ago, a number of persons of this description actually abandoned the anti-slavery lest by giving their influence in that direction they might possibly be giving countenance to the dangerous heresy that women, in respect to rights, stands on an equal footing with man. In the judgment of such persons the American slave system, with all its concomitant horrors is less to be destroyed than this wicked idea."[16]

There was one woman whom Elizabeth Cady Stanton and others wanted to invite to the convention also and that was Margaret Fuller but by

---

[16] History of Woman Suffrage, v. 1, p. 74 and Appendix

that time she had been killed in a boating accident. She was born in 1810 in New England. Her father was a lawyer and politician and had graduated from Harvard. She was taught by her father who even though she was a woman, he insisted that she be knowledgeable about all the subjects which he knew. By the age of six, she knew Latin; by eight, she knew French, Italian and Greek and in her early teens, German. Not only did she know the languages, but she read literature from all of them; her father treated her as an equal and companion.

But she became high strung and had depression. Her father learned he had pushed too much and too hard and trying to help, he sent her to a boarding school. Her education was so far advanced of the others that she was an outcast there. After two years she came home, and the family moved out to a farm never having been farmers. It was too much, and her mother broke down and her father died. She became the caretaker and took a job as teacher in Boston and then Providence to support the family. It was too staid for her and she needed an occupation that would use her education.

She started what was called "Conversations" where people paid to learn knowledge and speak well. There were thirteen sessions two hours each on various topics; the fee was large. This program lasted five years, Margaret was a gifted conversationalist and was well organized. She forced them to speak, organize their thoughts and make decisions; most had never done this before. Some of these women became involved with the suffrage movement and were very helpful for the organization.

There were a group of people known as the Transcendentalists who were free thinkers including people like Henry David Thoreau, Ralph Waldo Emerson, Bronson Alcott, and George and Sarah Ripley. Her sister married Henry David Thoreau and the Ripley's started Brook Farm. **The Dial** was a publishing forum which Margaret started along with Emerson as co-editor. Here she introduced feminist articles which evolved into a book called <u>Woman in the Nineteenth Century</u>. It stressed that women should be regarded as thinking individuals and all occupations should be open to them and not to be educated just to be good wives and mothers. The book, along with Mary Wollstonecraft made a big impact on women.

Margaret was the first woman on the staff of Horace Greeley's **New York Times,** doing in-depth stories on hospitals, prisons, and other necessary reforms.

In 1845 she wrote, "We would have every path open to Woman as freely as to man. . .Inward and outward freedom for Woman as much as for Man shall be acknowledged as a right, not yielded as a concession. . .Man cannot by right lay even well-meant restrictions on Woman.. . .What Woman needs is not as a woman to act or rule, but as a nature to grow, as an intellect to discern, as a soul to live freely and unimpeded, to unfold such powers as were given her."[17]

The last four years she spent in Italy involved in the Roman Republic revolution. There she met an Italian Marchese, fell in love, and married him secretly. They had a child and decided to come back to the United States as she was interested in the suffrage movement here. On the return voyage just as they were close to land, a huge gale swept over their ship and grounded it on a sandbar. It swept away the lifeboats and in attempting to reach shore, all of them drowned. She was considered one of the most educated and greatest speakers ever known. Her expertise probably would have greatly helped the suffrage movement and the opinion about women even more than it already had accomplished.

The two important women at Seneca Falls were Lucretia Mott and Elizabeth Cady Stanton; they had discussed this idea of suffrage in London and coordinated the effort of the Seneca Falls

[17] Ladies of Seneca Falls, p. 70

convention.   Let me begin with Lucretia Mott as she was the oldest and most experienced in speaking at this time. Here is her history.

She was born on January 3, 1793 and died on November 11,1880 working to the end for women's rights. She was Lucretia Coffin of a Quaker family. The tenets of Quakers included individualism, pacifism which meant they did not believe in war, equality of sexes and opposition to slavery. She was a cousin of the framer of the Constitution, Benjamin Franklin. They lived in Nantucket, Rhode Island; her father was a whaler; he spent much of his time even years away from the family.

Being Quakers, they let women speak in church and participate in the church. But Quakers did not vote in government elections. Because of her father's occupation and long absences, her mother opened a store and ran it buying the supplies and keeping the accounts. She made money from the store which eventually allowed the family to move to Boston.

Her father also believed that girls should get an education thus Lucretia had an opportunity to learn. She even became a minister herself when she was twenty-eight. All the children went to public school and Lucretia went to a Quaker school; she learned so fast and so well that at fifteen, she was asked to teach the younger children. James Mott was at the school and when the family moved to Philadelphia, he followed.

It was there that Lucretia married him in 1831 and they had six children and a good marriage. Lucretia and John became abolitionists and worked for the cause even having a place where the slaves could stay securely before moving on to the next place and eventually Canada. It was called a station on the Underground Railroad helping slaves escape to freedom. She became very influential and helped others to do the same; the Grimke' sisters were one of those who learned from Lucretia Mott. They were from South Carolina and had been slave owners but sold them all when their father died and became abolitionists instead. They spent the rest of their lives working against slavery.

The Mott home was often filled with guests such as William Lloyd Garrison, Wendell Phillips, Theodore Parker, and slaves moving north to Canada.

William Lloyd Garrison started the Anti-Slavery society in Philadelphia in 1839; Lucretia was not allowed to speak so she started the Female Anti-Slavery Society along with Garrison who strongly believed in women's rights too; this group formed in 1840. Wendell Phillips also believed in women's rights and joined Garrison.

In 1840, a World Anti-Slavery meeting was to be held in London, England and Lucretia Mott was chosen as the woman representative along with four men. When they arrived at the meeting, Lucretia was not recognized as a delegate nor allowed to speak. Not allowed to speak by the males particularly the ministers, she was forced to sit on the balcony away from the meeting behind a curtain.

They used the Bible as their authority saying that women were in subjection to men as that was the "will of God". How ironic that the meeting's object was gaining freedom for the slaves, but it was agreeable that women were subjects to do the will of men and not have any rights.

William Lloyd Garrison could not make it in the beginning but arrived four days later and because Lucretia Mott was not allowed to participate, he sat in the balcony with her. Seated also in the balcony with her was a newly married woman who had come with her husband, Henry, also an abolitionist. Her name was Elizabeth Cady Stanton; she and Lucretia became quick friends. They would take walks or go to eat and talking about women's rights. Both women were small; Lucretia had straight brown hair, a high forehead and always wore a gray and white Quaker dress with a hat. They both went back home but kept in contact with one another.

Lucretia and Elizabeth were well read and studied many new ideas. Both had read Mary Wollstonecraft's book <u>A Vindication of the Rights of Woman</u> and endorsed the Temperance Union. Lucretia Mott would also help start a women's college called Swarthmore in 1864 along with Joseph Wharton. Another well- known suffragist or I should say suffragette which means she was part of a militant group by the name of Alice Paul also attended there. The college still stands today.

Elizabeth Cady Stanton was the second woman responsible for the Seneca Falls convention; she is considered as a founder of the Woman's Rights movement. She was born November 12, 1815 in Johnstown, New York of a wealthy family involved in the fur trade with John Jacob Astor; she died October 24, 1902 in New York, New York. Her father was Judge Daniel Cady, a distinguished lawyer and a member of the New York legislature having great reserve and dignity. He was typical of men in that age that believed daughters should learn skills to be a housewife and not get an education.

She learned at an early age that she was not equal to men and felt the Scotch Presbyterian church certainly made her feel like she did nothing right. "The first event engraved in my memory was the birth of a sister when I was four years old. . . I heard so many friends remark 'What a pity it is she's a girl'. . . I did not understand at that time that girls were considered an inferior order of being".[18]

There was a minister in her town, Dr. Hossack, who talked to her and even taught her Greek. He told her girls were just as important as boys. She attended Johnstown Academy where she learned mathematics, Greek, and Latin. She rose to the top of her class even against the boys winning an award for the highest grades. Presenting the award to her father to hopefully win his praise, he just said he wished she was a boy. She had lost her brother, Eleazar, who was the only boy in the family, and her father was grieving over that; he did not give much praise to her achievements.

Even though he did not value girls, he realized her ability and let her visit him at his office and sit in on discussions since many of his clients were women having problems with their husbands. Husbands who had taken their wife's money and gambled or drank it away. Or the husbands who gave all his wife's money to his son which was the law, but the son gave her little support to the mother, who in many cases was destitute.

Elizabeth asked her father to do something and he just showed her the laws and told her to do

---

[18] Eighty Years and More, p. 4, Ladies of Seneca Falls, p. 56

something about when she grew up. When she did, he was proud of her actions but did not want her to be in public. She did get her father to send her to the Troy Female Seminary started by Emma Willard who believed in education for women but did not want suffrage for women. She had courses in mathematics, geography, and natural science but Elizabeth had learned these at Johnstown. She also did not like the all-girls school and became a supporter for co-education.

Every year their family visited a wealthy cousin, Gerrit Smith, who was also involved in the abolitionist movement. He was one of the richest landowners in New York state and lived at Peterborough. His only daughter, also Elizabeth, was Stanton's best friend. His home was a station on the Underground Railroad. She enjoyed the atmosphere of discussion and meeting interesting people.

One of these people was Henry Stanton who was ten years older than Elizabeth. They became involved and he proposed to her but her parents, particularly her father, objected. Henry had little money and when he married her, he would be in control of her money. He was also an abolitionist and Daniel Cady objected to that too; there were many discussions about his proposal and eventually

Elizabeth broke off the engagement although she kept writing to him.

In 1840, Henry also became a delegate to the World Anti-Slavery convention in London, England. He came back to Johnstown and asked Elizabeth to marry him which she did this time even though her father still objected. Getting a daughter married off was usually considered good.

They were married but Elizabeth refused to have the word obey in the ceremony nor did she follow the normal custom of taking her husband's first name as part of her title. She called herself Elizabeth Cady Stanton not Mrs. Henry Stanton.

They went to London but stopped off at friends of Henry. Their names were Theodore and Angelina Weld and her sister Sarah and other abolitionist friends. Angelina and Sarah were the Grimke' sisters who had been helped by Lucretia Mott and had become frequent anti-slavery speakers learning how to deal with people who did not want women speaking in public.

In London she met Lucretia Mott when the women had to sit in the balcony. They became acquainted and found out they had much to discuss not only about the abolitionist movement but about the treatment of women. They decided that they would meet again when they returned to the United States.

When they got back to the United States, Henry gave up being an abolitionist to please his father-in-law and became a lawyer instead. Daniel Cady bought them a house in Chelsea, New York. Visitors to their home included Stephen Foster and his wife Abbey, both of whom were abolitionist speakers, Frederick Douglass, an ex-slave, John Greenleaf Whittier, Ralph Waldo Emerson and Nathaniel Hawthorne. Elizabeth enjoyed the efforts made to work on reforms and the lively discussions held in various houses. Elizabeth also worked to gather signatures for the Married Woman's Act. This would allow women to keep money that they inherited.

In 1842, their first child Daniel was born; he was one of five boys and two girls. Taking care of seven children left little free time. She could not travel and speak at other places because she was having children and had to stay home and take care of them. In 1847, Henry moved his family to Seneca Falls because of his health. It was a smaller place with fewer social activities; Elizabeth became discontented with only the children as company and having to do most of the housekeeping chores as there were few people available in Seneca Falls. Henry was often away from home on business.

So that is where the first woman's convention was held as Elizabeth Stanton was already living there. Three hundred people met in Wesleyan Chapel including thirty-two men like William Lloyd Garrison and Frederick Douglass who had believed in giving rights to women along with Sojourner Truth, another ex-slave.

Martha Coffin Wright, born in 1806, was the sister of Lucretia Mott. She was also an abolitionist and spent twenty years traveling and speaking in favor of suffrage and against slavery. She was a close friend and supporter of Harriet Tubman. She was head of several conventions and was very active in the organization. She was president of NAWSA (National American Woman Suffrage Association) in 1874.

Mary Ann McClintock was born September,1849 and died on December 2, 1925; she worked in the abolitionist and suffrage movements also. She lived in Waterloo, New York close to Jane Hunt. They had rented property from Richard Hunt and both families were stations on the Underground Railroad. She had seven children who would follow in her footsteps working against slavery.

The meeting to organize the convention was held at the home of Jane and Richard Hunt. She was the wife of the richest man in Seneca County.

They were anti-slavery and became advocators of suffrage also. They were Hicksite Quakers who believed that men and women should discuss and run the church together. All five women met here in 1848 to discuss women's suffrage and all would sign the Declaration of Sentiments. The Quaker women were well experienced in strategy and tactics for organizing and running organizations from their work in the abolitionist movement.

Although Susan B. Anthony was not at Seneca Falls, her later influence makes her a definite part of the Women's Rights movement; She met Elizabeth Cady Stanton in 1851 and those two became the backbone of the suffrage movement along with Lucretia Mott. Susan was born February 15, 1820 one of eight children. She was also of a Quaker family as was Lucretia Mott. Susan's father, Daniel Anthony, said girls were as important as boys. He gave them a good education and taught them to be self-reliant and self- supporting and that girls could handle advanced education.

The Anthony Family heard the women's rights speakers in Rochester, New York and were inspired by what they heard and told Susan about it. Her father, mother, and sister attended having been invited by a cousin who was secretary of the convention. Her father was a sixth generation

Quaker but was very progressive in his thinking. That's why he gave his girls an education.

At the time, Susan was teaching at Canajoharie Academy and dropped the Quaker style of dress and had an active social life dating and getting involved in the temperance movement. She became an officer and gave a speech. After a few years, she became dissatisfied with teaching because as a woman she was paid $2.50 a week and a man for the same work was paid $10.00. She began to see the inequality of women and men firsthand. She had lived with a married cousin, Margaret Caldwell, who had lots of marital troubles that she could do nothing about as she had no rights. She passed away and Susan Anthony was very distressed over the conditions under which she had lived.

Susan returned home to her family home. They had gone through economic troubles when her father lost the farm, and everything was sold even her mother's things which she had gotten from her family. Josh, who was her uncle, had bought some of the family items and gave them back to her mother.

Because of the practice of taking a wife's money or belongings for the payment of debts, the parents of Lucy Anthony had set up a trust for her so that the money could not be used to pay Daniel

Anthony's debts. Her brother Josh was in control of the money until such time when it would be free of being taken again. This was the way that money could be protected from the laws that took everything from the married woman.

They had also had a failed cotton mill. He tried other jobs and lost another mill and he went back to farming. Josh bought the farm for the Anthony's but kept it in his name. At this point Daniel Anthony asked Susan to come back and manage the farm and as she was bored with just teaching, she agreed to manage the farm. For two years she spent time planting, harvesting, and getting the crops to market. The Married Woman's Act passed in 1848 and Josh proceeded to transfer the farm to Lucy Anthony.

Her father became an insurance salesman which proved a wise decision; he proceeded to make a prosperous living. He was also an abolitionist and a good friend of William Garrison and Wendell Phillips who were often at the abolitionist meetings; Susan also was well acquainted with them as was Elizabeth Stanton, but they had not met each other yet. Her father had made the farm a station on the Underground Railroad. Susan had a desire to get involved with the temperance movement. As Daniel was doing well financially, he agreed to let her do it and he gave her money. She became president of the anti-temperance movement in Rochester, New York.

Women who were bored or dissatisfied with domestic life joined the temperance organizations. Susan was president of the organization and there she met Amelia Bloomer who asked her to come to a Seneca Falls meeting in October; William Lloyd Garrison was the speaker at the meeting and it was after the meeting that in walking home Susan Anthony met Elizabeth Cady Stanton who liked her immediately. They went to her home and talked of women's rights, anti-slavery, and temperance. At that meeting was another lady, Lucy Stone, who was interested in both temperance and suffrage and had been speaking for both groups.

In 1852 Susan Anthony attempted to speak at a temperance meeting but was told women were not allowed to speak in public. Susan Anthony started a woman's temperance union with her as president and Elizabeth Stanton as secretary. Stanton wrote a speech saying women had the right to divorce a man who drank or abused the family, and married women had the right to their property and not have it sold to pay the husband's debts. Elizabeth Cady Stanton was the only woman who wanted divorce and incompatibility included in rights for women. Most women disagreed with this philosophy thinking it was too bold.

I have described the history of all these women as they became involved in the history of women and suffrage. Notice the characteristics of each of them and how similar they were in their actions. Lucretia Mott had mentioned the idea of how getting an education was vital to women to increase self -worth and alleviate her inferiority. All these women had educations that they worked mostly to get themselves. They were able to think, speak and write about how they felt and put it into action.   They followed this course throughout the suffrage movement.

ORGANIZATION AND NATIONAL WOMEN CONVENTIONS

Charging a Hat or Coat

The first National Women's convention occurred in Worcester, Massachusetts with representatives from eleven states. The year was 1850.

The 1850 National Women's Convention in Worcester, Massachusetts had 900 people present on October 23-24 with Paulina Wright Davis as the president. All the meetings began with and ended with prayers. All that the women had learned through meetings and discussions would now be put into action. These were the leaders and speakers who assembled and started the first conventions in 1848. With so many people there, people had to have attended other meetings and were filled with eagerness and resolve to make changes.

Speakers included Ernestine Rose, Antoinette Brown, who had been at Oberlin College with Lucy Stone, Abby Foster Kelley (an abolitionist also), Lucretia Mott, Paulina Wright Davis, Sojourner Truth, and Abby Price. Elizabeth Stanton was unable to come being in late pregnancy and Susan

Anthony had not yet joined the suffrage cause. Besides the addresses and speeches, resolutions were offered and discussed and perhaps adopted. It was early in the organization and the structure was developing. Rules of order were used throughout the meetings.

William Lloyd Garrison and Frederick Douglass were also there solidifying the abolitionists and suffrage groups. Lucy Stone only spoke the second day. Many reporters attended and mostly criticized the events though Horace Greeley gave fair reports which he printed up and the ladies used them as pamphlets to advertise women rights.

One woman who came for the first time at the 1850 convention was Ernestine Rose, a Jewish abolitionist and suffragist. She was born January 13, 1810 to a wealthy family in Poland. Her father was a rabbi and often fasted to show his dedication to his faith, but it left him sickly and weak.

Ernestine studied the Bible a lot when she was young and often asked questions and was told "little girls must not ask questions" and her retort was "little girls ask questions as well as girls"[19] Her mother died when Ernestine was sixteen, and her father remarried a year later. He arranged a marriage for her, but Ernestine refused the offer and lost her dowry which her mother had arranged for

[19] 19. History of Woman Suffrage, v. 1, p. 95

her. She sued for the right to have it but in the end left it with her father and traveled.

She traveled throughout Europe to Poland, Russia, the Germanic States, Holland, Belgium, France, and England. In England she met a reformer by the name of Robert Owen and through him, William Rose. William Rose was a jeweler and the two became acquainted and fell in love and married. The couple came to the United States and became citizens here.

Ernestine became very interested in suffrage and the abolition of slavery. She personally got a petition started and got five signatures for the Married Woman's Property Act in New York. She became acquainted with Elizabeth Stanton and Susan Anthony and they ended up very close and involved with suffrage. She worked tirelessly and traveled to twenty-three states giving speeches on woman's rights and abolition. She was president of the fifth convention in Philadelphia October 17-19, 1854. She was at all the conventions through 1869. Then she and her husband moved back to England where she stayed till her death even though Elizabeth Stanton and Susan Anthony traveled to England trying to persuade her to return to the U.S. and work for suffrage; their mission was unsuccessful.

Paulina Wright was a widow who had been left money by her husband. She used the money to work for women's rights. She gave lectures on physiology and anatomy and even had a plaster figure of the anatomy of a woman which she used in her lectures to show what she was teaching. Women didn't know such things and were considered unable to comprehend and too delicate to hear such things. Here was yet another woman who was educated in physical science who mastered the subjects and taught them to women.

Susan Anthony was still not at the 1851 convention as she was still working with the Temperance Union. But when she went to the meetings, she was not allowed to speak, being a woman, as she was told by the presiding officer. She asked Elizabeth Stanton to help her with a Woman's Temperance speech and Mrs. Stanton agreed but said that Susan Anthony might not like her speech thinking it too radical because she recommended women divorce their alcoholic husbands.

The Industrial Revolution brought about mills for making cloth. This started in 1830. Of the around 58,000 people who worked in the factories, 40,000 were women. They worked in towns and lived in dorms provided by the owners. They were paid $l.75 a week or $.35-.37a day of which $l.45 went to the owner of the dorms. They lived in rooms with twelve others and worked from twelve to sixteen hours a day and they saw very little, if any of the money they earned. Although the women working in the factories did not, at first, work for suffrage, they would do so later in the movement. They organized into trade groups and would in later years be just as active.

In too many marriages, the money was not used for anything except what the husband wanted, and these women were abused and submissive and gave up hope. Even women whose husbands provided for them did not have money to spend themselves. The argument used against women suffrage was that men were supposed to take care of the women but in most cases, they were left with little or nothing. And this is what women learned as they came to the suffrage meetings. It's also why there were four meetings in 1850; women were more and more interested in learning about what to do and became supporters; they were starving for answers about how to free themselves from their burdens.

At Seneca Falls four women were Quakers. It was from this background that Lucretia Mott came to the meeting and why she was doubtful about including voting in the resolutions. Susan B. Anthony was also a Quaker although she had turned from it so was more welcoming to the idea of suffrage. The latter Quaker was Alice Paul who was very adamant about getting women the right to vote through a congressional passage of an amendment added to the Constitution.

Elizabeth Stanton and Lucy Stone believed in giving women the right to vote. The first strong leaders already had differing opinions about voting for women and the way to achieve this goal. It caused discussion and compromise among them and would lead to different groups with opposite views being formed in attempting to gain suffrage for women. The compromises also led to mostly leaving out African American women in the suffrage movement because the original founders wanted the southern women to join the suffrage movement and work for that goal and they wouldn't work if African women were allowed; it was a bad mark against the movement.

Lucy Stone Blackwell

The 1851 National Rights convention was also held in Worcester, Massachusetts at Brimley Hall on October 15 and 16. The speakers were mostly the same as in 1850 except Elizabeth Oakes Smith was added as a speaker. Elizabeth was a journalist born in 1806 and a radical women's rights spokeswoman which is why she was at the national convention. Most of her writings were under pen names or pseudonyms as women were not considered competent or intelligent to write. She wrote and published all her life; she was also married and had six sons. She lived with one of them after her husband died in 1869.

At most of the conventions held, a small fee was charged to pay for the expenses because the locations were not donated. This was in the time before planes, cell phones, and cars that women made the effort to travel to the convention. There were three times the number as in 1848. It took a lot of effort and expense to be there, but they came because they had determination. They walked, rode horseback, came by train or carriages or any way that was the cheapest and easiest for them to get there.

There were speeches given and letters read by speakers such as Angelina Grimke' Weld, Ralph Waldo Emerson, Horace Mann, Henry Ward Beecher, and Francis Gage. Men who supported suffrage attended many of the meetings, men such as Wendell Phillips, Gerrit Smith, Frederick Douglass, and William Lloyd Garrison.

Elizabeth Stanton was not there again but her letter was read; she was a very prolific writer. The possibility of setting up a national committee was discussed but not approved. In each convention the steps of progress were enumerated to the delegates on the progress of suffrage. This was the purpose of the convention to keep the delegates up to date and to instill purpose to their cause.

Minutes were kept of all the conventions but on top of that everything that was spoken or read was incorporated into record so there was a complete and accurate account of what happened at each meeting. Even though suffrage was not one of these, many other smaller freedoms were introduced and made as part of the law. Women were slowly tearing down the barriers of women in the country.

Sojourner Truth had been born into slavery in 1797 in New York and became free in 1827. She began to speak out against slavery and became a frequent extemporaneous speaker. She could neither read nor write nor did she ever learn but speaking out was not a problem. In 1851 in Akron, Ohio, she delivered her famous "Ain't I a Woman".

She had endured the miseries of being a slave being beaten and sold. After escaping Isabella Baumtree changed her name to Sojourner and became an itinerant preacher and got involved in the anti-slavery organization. She was around six feet tall and she worked for the anti-slavery cause and for suffrage.

Sojourner Truth

This was her speech in response to another speaker saying women were expected to be taken care of by men. I am giving you two versions of her speech. This one was recorded by Frances Dana Gage recorded in 1863 years after the speech. It was recorded into History of Woman Suffrage as Frances Gage was a member. "I tink dat twixt de niggers of the souf and de womin of the norf all talkin 'bout rights de white men will be in a fix. But whats all dis here talkin 'bout ? Dat man ober dar say that womin needs to be helped into carriages and lifted over ditches and to hav the best place everwhar. Nobody eber helps me into carriages or ober mud puddles or givs me any best place   And ain't I a woman. Look at me! Look at my arm! I have ploughed and planted and gathered into barns and no man could head me! I could work as much and eat as much as a man-when I could get it-and bear the lash as well! And ain't I a woman? I have bourne 13 children and see em mos all sold off to slavery, and when I cried out with my mother's grief, none but Jesus hear me! And ain't I a woman..................Den dat little man in black dar say women cant have as much rights as men caus Christ wasn't a woman! Whar did your Christ come from? From God and a woman! Man had nothin' to do wid him!"[20]

The second speech was recorded by Reverend Marius Robinson who was a friend of Sojourner Truth. It was published June 21, 1851 in the Anti-Slavery Bugle several weeks later after Sojourner had given the speech. He talked with her about what she had said to make sure he was accurate.

Sojourner had been a slave, but she was from New York and would have had a Dutch dialect.

[20] History of Woman Suffrage, v. 1., p. 116

"May I say a few words? I want to say a few words about this matter. I am a woman's rights. I have as much muscle as any man and can do as much work as any man.

I have plowed and reaped and husked and chopped and mowed, and can any man do more than that? I have heard much about the sexes being equal; I can carry as much as any man and can eat as much too, if I can get it. I am as strong as any man that is now.

As for intellect, all I can say is, if women have a pint and man a quart-why can't she have her little pint full? You need not be afraid to give us our rights for fear we will take too much, but we can't take more than our pint'll hold.

The poor man seem to be all in confusion, and don't know what to do.

Why children, if you have woman's rights, give it to her and you will feel better. You will have your rights, and they won't be so much trouble. I can't read, but I can hear. I have heard the Bible and have learned that Eve caused man to sin.

Well if woman upset the world, do give her a chance to set it right side up again. The lady has spoken about Jesus, how he never spurned woman from him, and she was right. When Lazarus died, Mary and Martha came to him with faith and love and besought him to raise their brother. And Jesus wept and Lazarus came forth.

And how came Jesus into the world? Through God who created him and woman who bore him. Man, where is your part? But the women are coming up blessed be God and a few of the men are coming up with them. But man is in a tight place, the poor slave is on him, woman is coming on him, and he is surely between a hawk and a buzzard."[21]

Other Africans who worked for the suffragist movement and abolition included the Forten family. James Forten was an African American abolitionist and wealthy businessman born a free man in Philadelphia, Pennsylvania home of where the Constitution was written. His parents were also wealthy. He married and had eight children. Because they were wealthy, they did not attend the public schools but had private teachers at home. When they grew up, they worked arduously in the abolitionist movement and having stations for the underground railroad. They were free but worked for those not free.

His daughter, Charlotte, joined the Anti-Slavery society and became a teacher in a school for both blacks and whites. She taught during the

[21] Library of Congress Link to Sojourner Truths speech "Aint I a Woman" recorded by Marcus Robinson in Anti-Slavery Bugle in 1851

Civil War and helped take care of soldiers in Port Royal, South Carolina. She married Francis Grimke', a minister and author who spoke out for civil rights of blacks and worked to get them the right to vote after the Civil War. He was the nephew of the Grimke' sisters.

Margaretta Forten also the daughter of James Forten, was an abolitionist and suffragist who was responsible for helping to start The Philadelphia Anti-Female Society in 1833 along with her mother and sisters Sarah and Harriet. Others including Lucretia Mott joined in this effort when they were not allowed in the original all male group. African Americans who were not allowed in the formed suffragist groups founded their own including the National Association of Colored Women by Ida B. Wells.

In 1852 the National Women's Rights convention was held September 8-10 in Syracuse, New York. Lucretia Mott was president and Martha Wright was secretary. Elizabeth Cady Stanton, again, sent a letter in her absence. Her letter proposed divorce for a woman whose husband was a drunk and abused her; it was not accepted. Susan Anthony attended her first National Woman's Rights convention and gave her first speech along with Matilda Joslyn Gage who was the youngest speaker at a convention.

She met Lucretia Mott, Martha Wright, Ernestine Rose, Antoinette Brown, and Paulina Wright Davis, and Lucy Stone who wore a bloomer costume created by Amelia Bloomer in Seneca Falls. Elizabeth Smith Miller, daughter of Gerrit Smith and cousin of Elizabeth Cady Stanton, had brought it back from Europe and wore it for years though Amelia Bloomer actually made the clothing and was given the credit. It was a comfortable piece of clothing that was a divided skirt; it did not need to have tight underclothes to wear it and did not drag on the ground. Other suffragists also wore it for a while, but women gave up personal comfort for political reasons. It was used in later years as a costume for gym and skating.

There were over 2, 000 people there from over eight states and Canada. The word of the suffrage meetings was spreading, and the women were willing to travel to speak and listen to the struggle that most women had. More and more women realized they were not alone in fighting for the injustice imposed upon women. A resolution to have a national organization was defeated. There were many more who knew nothing of what was going on because they could not read or write. By the end of the meeting, Susan Anthony had committed herself to the woman's rights movement.

In 1853 the meeting was in Cleveland, Ohio on October 6-8 with Dana Francis Gage presiding. Over 1500 people attended. There was a resolution to prepare a new Declaration of Rights, but it was voted down. Newspaper accounts depicted the delegates as being thin unattractive maiden ladies who had been rejected by men and were bitter. Truthfully, most of the women in the suffrage movement were married.

As at most meetings there was much discussion of policy and resolutions as how to achieve the rights of women. An example of the hundreds of such resolutions brought up in the conventions is "resolved, that for the men of this land-- to claim for themselves the elective franchise, and the right to choose their own rulers and enact their own laws, as essential to their freedom, safety, and welfare, and then to deprive all the women of all these safeguards, solely on the ground of a different sex is to evince the pride of self-esteem, the meanness of usurpation, and the folly of a self-assumed superiority-That woman, as well as man, has a right to the highest mental and physical development; to the most ample educational advantages; to the occupancy of whatever position she can reach".[22] This type of resolution was introduced at every convention that women had the

---

[22] History of Woman's Suffrage, v.1, p.518

right to vote, to carry on their own business and to be able to choose their education and jobs and keep their wages which would be equal to the men.

In 1854 the meeting on October 18,19, and 20th was held in Sansom Hall in Philadelphia, Pennsylvania. Ernestine Rose was the president of this meeting. Lucretia Mott, Amy Post, and Martha Coffin Wright were the presiders of the convention. Amy Post had been one of the three organizers at the second women's meeting in 1848 at Rochester.

Elizabeth Stanton was the speaker; her topic was about marriage being domestic servitude and that women should have the right to divorce. Women had no rights to money, so they had to endure these conditions.

Talks at this convention included reports of the legislative victory in New York of the reforms of the Married Woman's Act which now allowed joint custody of children and wives having the sole use of property that they inherited and wages that they earned. A second resolution to have a national organization was defeated and the delegates decided to support local and state efforts for suffrage.

There were around 600-800 people present at the meeting. As you can read, the people who were consistently at the early conventions were Lucretia

Mott, Martha Wright, Lucy Stone, and Susan Anthony. Elizabeth Stanton was behind the scenes doing a lot of writing. The original intent was to have the conventions in various states so the delegates could appear before the legislatures of those states since they allowed various groups that right. It became a better idea to keep the conventions close to the Congress of the United States so that the women could appear and speak before the legislative committees and even before the House of Representatives and the Senate.

It will be Elizabeth Stanton and Susan Anthony who will forge the women's rights movement for fifty years. Elizabeth did much of the writing and Susan would be the organizer. She was also the person who raised money, procured meeting sites, and kept in touch with the other suffragists; that's why she was referred as "Aunt Susan". Susan was the better speaker, but Elizabeth was the best writer and Susan would give the speeches very timidly at the beginning, but she gained confidence. Elizabeth had her seven children and could not get away from the children; she would complain about it and Susan would go out to her house and help take care of the children while Elizabeth rested or worked on reform speeches. With so many children, it was hard to find quiet time and they were noted for being very active. The children became so used to having her around that they considered her part of the family and also called her "Aunt Susan" and they frequently went to the Anthony farm in Rochester, New York. Susan B. Anthony became an excellent speaker out of necessity becoming very comfortable and adept in doing this.

Susan B. Anthony

The two of them would work together on speeches, goals, and organization. When they could arrange it, the two would travel together giving speeches and talking to women and attending the legislative sessions.

Between conventions, individual women did what they could. Lucy Stone lectured on women's rights; Amelia Bloomer worked on the woman's paper she started called **The Lily** while Paulina Wright Davis worked with **The Una.** Lucretia Mott also went out lecturing and urging other women to attend conventions, to petition legislators, write speeches and anything to inform women as did Martha Wright, Lucretia's sister who worked as much as she did but who was not as well known. Susan Anthony attended every New York State Teachers convention forcing the men to allow women take part in the proceedings.

The 1855 convention was October 17 and 18 in Cincinnati, Ohio with the president being Martha Coffin Wright, who was also there with Josephine Griffing, Ernestine Rose, Lucy Stone and her new husband, Henry Blackwell. The purpose of this meeting as in the others was to secure equal, political, and civil rights for women. Again, there were speeches and discussion, resolutions that were discussed and then voted either for or against. This was the normal routine of these national conventions. By this time, the newspapers were reporting on their meetings with little comment whereas originally, they commented on the meetings with disdain. Elizabeth Cady Stanton had given a speech before a joint judiciary committee of both houses and was the first woman to be allowed to do so.

The national convention of 1856 was held in New York City at the Broadway Tabernacle on November 25-26. Lucy Stone presided over the meeting. A letter from Antoinette Brown was delivered with the recommendation of working in the state legislatures to get suffrage votes was passed. Elizabeth Stanton's letter again recommended divorce as a solution for the problems of divorce and alcoholism in marriages and it was again rejected.

There was no convention in 1857.

In 1858 on May 13 and 14, the convention was held in New York City and Susan B. Anthony presided. She had become a dominant worker for suffrage. This meeting also coincided with the Anti-Slavery meeting being held which became a joint meeting of interested parties. There were over 1,000 people there. The business again concerned getting information out to women to educate them on what was being done and to the legislatures of the states to persuade them to introduce needed legislation. An anonymous donor gave $5,000 to be given to suffrage under the trust of Wendell Phillips to be used for paying for lectures, tracts, pamphlets, and the expenses involved with meetings regarding suffrage. He invested it wisely and almost doubled its value.

The 1859 convention in New York City again was held only on May 12. Lucretia Mott presided over this one day. The speakers that one day were interrupted by the disruptive forces and opponents who were the anti-suffragists. They were vociferous and intended to keep up these actions to disrupt and antagonize. Along with the clergy, the suffragists realized they were their opponents, but they would not be the worst. The one good point was that Wendell Phillips gave the convention a donation from Charles H. Hovey in the amount of $8,000 to be divided among reform groups including the suffrage groups.

Elizabeth Stanton's father passed on in 1859 and left her $50,000 which would make her independent along with money she earned in speaking. She also had seven children which made it hard for her to be at meetings and conventions. As the children got older, she gained freedom to work for suffrage.

In 1860 on May 10 and 11th, the national convention was attended by 600 - 800 people with Martha Coffin Wright as presider. It was held at Association Hall in Albany, New York. Speeches given were discussed. A resolution was

introduced that would allow women to separate or divorce from husbands who were cruel, insane, drunk, abusive, or deserted their families. The consensus was that it was too controversial at this point of the movement and would alienate too many women and was defeated. Elizabeth Cady Stanton had introduced the subject of divorce since 1848 and ended up feeling that she had brought up the subject too early but in later years, it was accepted as a choice and not morally wrong.

Martha Wright

This was the last convention until after the Civil War. All the women at the convention felt the war should take precedence over suffrage except for Susan B. Anthony who wanted the conventions continued. Unfortunately, the conventions held after the war became divided by the two groups, AWSA (American Woman Suffrage Association) and NWSA (National Woman Suffrage Association.)

The format would be much the same with resolutions, discussion, and what actions to take but division split the effort given to suffrage. The number of suffragists kept increasing as did contributions to the group. By the 1900's membership had increased to 2,000,000 and the conventions were twice as long, and the suffrage movement had a permanent headquarters and a healthy budget. Women in the workforce had increased to over 7 million from less than three million and were seeking equal social rights so they organized into unions and joined the suffrage movement.

How do we know about all the discussions, speeches, and actions of the women at these yearly conventions? Because the women kept copious notes of everything said and discussed. They recorded all speeches, policies, procedures, activities of suffragists from all over the country and what representatives and delegates attended these yearly conventions. They would write it down for a permanent record. Susan B. Anthony and Elizabeth Cady Stanton along with Mathilda Gage would get together and organize and write the voluminous amount of information into volumes.

Harriet Stanton Blatch, daughter of Elizabeth Stanton also helped her mother and the others with writing this collection of books on the suffrage movement. Susan Anthony was the one responsible for keeping all the notes and record of speeches along with numerous clippings from newspapers and magazines. She organized them all and in preparation for writing. This lengthy and accurate history was called the History of Woman's Suffrage. Volume I covered the years 1848-1861; Volume II-1861-1876; Volume III-1876-1882; Volume IV-1883-1900.Two more were added with Susan B. Anthony and Elizabeth Stanton working on these with Ida Husted Harper to make a total of six. Volume V was from 1900-1920 and Volume VI was also from 1900-1920 covering suffrage in the other countries of the world.

It is a total of over 5,000 pages of information which recorded everything the suffragists had done for the entire period of the struggle to get women the right to vote. These volumes are available for everyone to have proof of what was done to get the vote and rights for women. Long, very long hours were given to this task along with traveling, petitions, and appearances before legislative committees and in front of the legislatures. Most if not all suffragists did this same thing. And you can google this entire series of books to read at your leisure.

THE CIVIL WAR AND SUFFRAGE

Charging a Hat or Coat

When the Civil War started in 1861, the women's rights people wanted to postpone future meetings until after the Civil War. They urged them to concentrate on ending slavery and getting them the right to vote but only the for the men. One of the leading proponents of this was Frederick Douglass saying the women's time would come after the slaves were free. Susan Anthony had refuted this argument but was outvoted by both Elizabeth Stanton and Lucretia Mott. They felt the war effort should be the major concern and for their efforts, they felt they would be given the right to vote. Elizabeth Stanton did have this to say about abolition, "To me there was no question so important as the emancipation of women from the dogmas of the past, political, religious, and social. It struck me as very remarkable that abolitionists, who felt so keenly the wrongs of the slave, should be so oblivious to the equal wrongs of their own mothers, wives, and sisters"[23]

---

[23] Ladies of Seneca Falls, p. 56

Although there were no women's conventions, the women worked throughout the war. The men were fighting so the women took over jobs that men had done. From this they gained more experience, boldness and learning to express their dissatisfaction with their lack of rights. They managed farms and businesses along with working in other jobs. Women also cooked, knitted, and sewed to help the soldiers.

The first organization formed was the Woman's Central Association of Relief on April 17,1861 to organize all volunteer groups. Dorothea Dix helped wounded soldiers saving over 180,000 lives. She was superintendent of nurses and nursing work was done by private donations. The women's groups raised millions of dollars to help provide for this effort. There was no national organization and no money to even provide for it.

Dr. Elizabeth Blackwell, sister-in-law of Lucy Stone Blackwell and Antoinette Brown Blackwell also a sister-in-law, recruited and trained thousands of nurses for the army hospitals. Antoinette had married Samuel, who was Henry's brother. Lucy and Antoinette had attended Oberlin together.

She organized The Sanitary Commission under government authority making bandages, packing boxes, gathering materials to get to the front, and raising $92 million in aid for the care of the sick and wounded. It was predicted that three-fourths of the soldiers died from lack of proper care of their wounds rather than actual battle death.

The Union Army was poorly organized and had no money or staff. They lost many battles in the beginning because of this fact. The Sanitary Commission not only raised the money but handled the finances. This was the forerunner of the Red Cross and the work was so well done that foreign observers were impressed by the Union effort. Clara Barton was responsible for much of this work. But the southern women worked just as hard for the Confederate cause.

One woman was a military heroine of the Civil War. Her name was Anna Ella Carroll. She was an adviser to President Lincoln, and to the Civil War commander Ulysses Grant. She was born August,1815 to a wealthy Maryland family. Her father was governor of Maryland and her grandfather was a signer of the Declaration of Independence. She was a politician, wrote pamphlets about the evils of slavery and helped them escape and get to safety. Abraham Lincoln considered her an asset to the Union cause. She was anti-slavery and freed her own slaves. She was a Lincoln supporter and convinced him of a military plan to invade the south through the Tennessee and Cumberland Rivers rather than the Mississippi. It was implemented and was successful, but it was kept secret. These victories helped Ulysses S. Grant achieve some of his early victories.

After the war, it was denied that she had anything to do with the operation and she was discredited because of the prejudice against her sex. She lived in dire poverty her last fifteen years of her life. Abraham Lincoln was already dead and could not collaborate her story. She was eventually exonerated although she died in destitution.

Women also held civic, political, and heads of departments during the Civil War. Ann Bickerdyke, a Quaker, went to the battlefield bringing supplies and nursing the wounded soldiers. Quakers did not believe in war and refused to fight but they were willing to help in other ways.

Salmon Chase, Secretary of the Treasury under Lincoln, had lost his young men to the draft or volunteering for the war effort. Needing workers, he hired women as clerks in various jobs in the government and they worked out well; he felt this had been one of the better jobs he had implemented during the war.

There were over 400 women soldiers, spies, and scouts that helped the cause. These women included Elizabeth Compton of the 25th Michigan Cavalry, Ellen Goodridge of Virginia, Sophia

Thompson, Josephine Davidson, and Frances Hook of Illinois to name a few. The people involved would cover an entire book.

Josephine Griffing help start the Freedman's Bureau that helped escaped slaves learn to read and write and found shelters for them. Elizabeth Keckley, a former slave, became the dressmaker for Mrs. Lincoln. Lucretia Mott and her husband James having worked so hard and long for the anti-slavery cause helped the former slaves by selling them plots of land from their farm to build homes.

The second organization that was started May 14, 1863 in New York City, New York was the Woman's National Loyal League. Lucy Stone Blackwell presided. Elizabeth Stanton was appointed as president and Susan B. Anthony as the secretary.

In the same year, Abraham Lincoln issued the Emancipation Proclamation, but it only freed the slaves in the seceded states not the border states which were Maryland, Delaware, Kentucky, and West Virginia which had divided from Virginia to stay in the Union rather than be in the Confederacy.

Since the women had suspended their suffrage fight, they spent the time gathering petitions to end slavery and for the passage of the 13th amendment. They sent over 400,000 signatures to Congress in 1864 which helped bring about the amendment in 1865. Charles Sumner, a Republican senator, presented the signatures to Congress. Susan Anthony had tried to get suffrage added to the 13ʰ Amendment but it was rejected.

Susan B. Anthony

At the same time Frances Ellen Watkins Harper advocated to bring the two causes of suffrage for the freed slaves and the enfranchisement of women both white and African as one cause; it was rejected. She was an African American and a strong abolitionist and suffragist. They did keep trying to get suffrage included in the legislative efforts.

The 14th amendment was passed in 1868 not without debate on including the word male for the first time in the amendment and the 15th amendment in 1870. The suffragists were against using the word male as it would further leave out women in suffrage. These two amendments would bring women back to their original focus of working for women rights and suffrage. The league gave valuable experience to the women in organization, networking and gathering petitions.

When the 14th amendment was proposed, Elizabeth Stanton and Susan Anthony wanted a resolution to include suffrage for all women, white and black but this was looked on with disfavor by both other women and antislavery men who had originally supported women's suffrage, men like Wendell Phillips, Gerrit Smith, and even Frederick Douglass. They said that now was not the time and to waive their demand for suffrage right now since they felt it was going hard just to get the vote for the black men. The phrase now is not the time was used frequently during this time and angered the suffrage people having worked so hard to help the abolitionists.

Elizabeth Cady Stanton said "We demand. . . suffrage for all the citizens of the Republic. I would not talk of negroes or women but of citizens."[24] The 14th amendment said in section 1 that "All persons born or naturalized in the United States and subject to the jurisdiction thereof, are citizens of the United States and of the states therein they reside. No state shall make or enforce any law which shall

[24] History of Woman's Suffrage, v. 2, p. 217

abridge the privileges or immunities of citizens of the United States nor shall any state deprive any persons of life, liberty or property, without due process of law, nor deny any person within its jurisdiction the equal protection of the laws." (Constitution) The amendment said all persons not any race or color or sex but all persons. By the simple description, that would mean that both men and women, white and black would not be deprived of their rights. The second section though used the word male which was the first time it had been included in the Constitution. In 1866 the women's rights groups sent resolutions to Congress to include suffrage in the amendments. Theodore Stevens, majority leader of the Senate, introduced this measure but it was rejected.

About the same time, the American Equal Rights Association was formed by Lucy Stone Blackwell and Susan B. Anthony with Lucretia Mott as president. Its goal was suffrage for all regardless of race, color, or sex. Frances Harper was also a leader of this group; she had been born a slave in Maryland and orphaned as a child. She got an education at her uncle's school and worked and spoke for the anti-slavery groups.

Men and women joined this group working and holding meetings but the difference of opinion about who would be voting and when it should be granted caused dissension. Men like Wendell Phillips insisted that the former slaves should have the vote first and then the women would get theirs in due time.

In 1867 Sojourner Truth said " there is a great stir about colored men getting their rights, and not a colored women theirs, and if colored men get their rights and not colored women theirs, you see the colored men will be masters over the women, and it will be just as bad as it was before."[25] Too many women felt that suffrage would be given to women after the Civil War as a reward for all their work and support during the war but that did not happen. In fact, what happened was they turned against the suffrage movement and concentrated on getting the rights for colored men. They told the women that if they waited, it would eventually come to women. That was not acceptable to the women.

Sojourner Truth

---

[25] History of Woman's Suffrage, v. 2, p. 193

The 15th Amendment stated "the rights of the citizens of the United States to vote shall not be denied or abridged by the United States or any state on account of race, color, or any previous condition of servitude. (Constitution) The amendment is simple and concise about voting which leads to its interpretation. The second section states that the Congress shall have the power of enforcement as it did in amendment 14th also. They wanted the word sex added after color, but this did not occur. But the women's rights groups will interpret both amendments as allowing voting.

In 1868 Elizabeth Cady Stanton and Susan B. Anthony published **The Revolution** as a method of keeping suffrage in the news. This was for the NWSA; it had now been twenty years since suffrage had been introduced. They were both discouraged by the lack of progress with suffrage and wanted a different venue to approach the effort. It ran for years accumulating a very large debt so it closed in 1870. Susan Anthony took on the responsibility of paying off the debt and did it in six years. She gave speeches to earn money and had help from individuals including her sister, Mary.

Paulina Wright Davis formed The New England Woman Suffrage Association headed by Lucy Stone Blackwell and Henry Blackwell in opposition to **The Revolution** and who had been associated with it. George Francis Train had donated to **The Revolution** cause but was considered a detriment as he was outspoken and considered a racist. It was also to support the Republicans who wanted voting rights for the African Americans.

Frederick Douglass

Their first speaker for that meeting was Frederick Douglass who said, "The cause of the negro is more pressing than that of women."[26]

In the convention of January 19 ,1869 colored men there denounced the women for jeopardizing

---

[26] History of Woman's Suffrage, v. 3, p. 324

their chance to vote saying as so many others had that God intended the male should dominate the female everywhere. This is what Sojourner Truth had said earlier. Susan B. Anthony had said at the beginning of the Civil War that the suffrage movement should continue so as not to be forgotten and that is what happened. Having achieved the amendments, suffrage was a moot point to the abolitionists. A division starts.

SPLIT OF SUFFRAGE INTO GROUPS

The two suffrage groups formed were the NWSA (National Woman Suffrage Association) and the AWSA (American Woman Suffrage Association). The NWSA was headed by Elizabeth Cady Stanton and Susan B. Anthony who wanted the right to vote as the main goal of the organization and to work specifically on that and only women should be included in the group. They also wanted other reforms for the rights of women which is what Stanton had been urging for years. They opposed the 15th Amendment because it did not include women in the writing but only male black men.

The AWSA was headed by Lucy Stone, Clara Foltz, Laura de Force Gordon, Julia Ward Howe, Louisa May Alcott, and Myra Bradwell. Men were also included in the group with Henry Blackwell and others. The **Woman's Journal** was the newspaper used by this group for giving information to the public. They were in favor of the 15th Amendment and wanted to lobby state legislatures for the women's right to vote.

Lucy Stone was born in 1818 in Brookline, Massachusetts. Her mother had to milk eight cows the day before Lucy was born as the men were out in the field saving a crop from the weather. Even though she was disabled, it was still expected of her as she was a woman. She did all the laundry even that of the hired help. She did the cooking and chores and helped physically on the farm of 145 acres.

Lucy rebelled against this treatment, but her mother said that women were being punished for what Eve did and must accept their treatment as tradition approved by the Bible. She called women the "daughters of Eve". This made her mother feel inferior and be submissive. Lucy was expected to do her fair share and even made shoes to sell. She could make nine pairs in a day that sold for the price of four cents each.

"Is the child crazy"? her father asked when she wanted to go to college. He paid for his sons to go but told Lucy she had to earn or borrow money to attend college which she did when she went to Oberlin College in 1843. The school accepted women and by the charter women could take all courses. She worked in the kitchen for $.03 an hour and was paid $1.25 a month in the preparatory school which was less than what men earned. Oberlin was also a station on the Underground Railroad.

Lucy took a rhetoric class along with Antoinette Brown (Blackwell)who was also attending Oberlin and graduated in 1850. She was in the theological seminary program, but they would not give her the theological degree. It was done later in 1878; she also was awarded a D.D. (Doctor of Divinity in 1908)

Women could write speeches or essays but were not allowed to read them out in class. The professor let both girls debate each other. Lucy was chosen by her class to write the graduating essay but was never allowed to give it herself.

She was the first Massachusetts woman to graduate from there and started giving speeches during the week on suffrage and anti-slavery on the weekends. She was not given a chance to speak in public but her brother, Bowman, gave her a chance to practice speaking in his church, and she became a popular extemporaneous speaker. She was characterized as a large woman who smoked cigars but in person, she was small and dressed neatly. The anti-slavery society used to give her $4.00 for speaking on the weekends. In the space of three years she earned $7,000.

She came to Rochester in 1858 for the anti-slavery convention but there was also the National Women's Rights Convention where she met Susan B. Anthony, Elizabeth Cady Stanton, Mr. and Mrs.

Wendell Phillips, James and Lucretia Mott, Ralph Waldo Emerson, Angelina Grimke', Sojourner Truth, and Paulina Wright Davis. Elizabeth Cady Stanton and Susan B. Anthony were considered radical but so had Lucy Stone been considered the same while at Oberlin.

All of them became friendly and Lucy focused on suffrage more. She married Henry Blackwell, keeping her maiden name just as Stanton did. They were married by Reverend Thomas Wentworth Higginson who supported suffrage and joined AWSA. Her viewpoint about how to obtain suffrage became different after the Civil War. The AWSA followed the idea of state by state suffrage and allowing men to belong to the group.

Clara Foltz, Laura de Force Gordon and Myra Bradford all members of AWSA were all three women who sought and achieved law degrees.

Clara was the first woman lawyer on the west coast; she was born July 16, 1849 and was the first public defender. Her family moved to Mt. Pleasant, Iowa prior to the Civil War. At fifteen, she eloped with Jeremiah Foltz in 1864. They moved first to Oregon, then San Jose, California. By then they had five children and Benjamin could not support them. Clara wrote articles for **The New Northwest**.

He then deserted her; she was left with five children to support. They had moved to California to seek their fortune; she got a job reading law at the office of a local judge and decided to become a lawyer. She applied to take the bar examination but was denied admission as she was a woman and not a white male. She, along with Laura de Force Gordon wrote a Woman Lawyer Bill replacing the words white male with person in 1871. It was granted in 1878. Passing the examination in 1878, she became the first woman admitted to the California Bar.

Later wanting to improve her skills, she applied to Hastings and was denied claiming the white male qualification again. Here she joined forces with Laura de Force Gordon, and they sued. They wrote an amendment to the California constitution leaving out the while male qualification and replacing it with person. The case went to the state Supreme Court and won the case in 1879. Clara and Laura became two women to practice law in California; Clara was the first woman lawyer in California to finish law school, join the bar, and practice law in California.

She was the first clerk of the State Assembly in 1880. She was on The Board of Corrections, a Notary Public, director of a major bank, a deputy

D.A. for the city of Los Angeles, and at 81 ran for governor of California in 1930.

Laura Gordon was born on August 17, 1838 in Pennsylvania. She was a suffragist, lawyer, and female publicist of a daily newspaper. She was considered to be a radical and spent time speaking for suffrage. She, along with Clara Foltz fought for women being admitted to the bar in California. She married Dr. Charles Gordon in New Orleans during the Civil War. They first moved to Nevada where she was the first white woman in 1867 after the Civil War.

Then they moved to California where she, too, worked for suffrage. Laura often traveled around California giving over 100 suffrage speeches. Her speech "The Elective Franchise, Who Shall Vote" was the first in California. It was not uncommon for many of the suffrage women to do the same thing. She started the California Suffrage Association in 1870. She also worked for the **Daily Democrat** and was a lobbyist. She also attended the National Woman's Convention in 1872.

On December 6, 1879 she was admitted to the State Bar of California; she was the second woman after Clara Foltz. By 1880, she had her own firm in San Francisco where she practiced general and criminal law and was the first woman to argue a case before a jury. She was also the second woman to be admitted to the U.S. Supreme Court after Belva Lockwood.

Mrs. Myra Bradwell was the third woman who applied to be admitted to the bar after she got her law degree in Illinois. She was denied admission and sued; the decision came on April 4. 1873. Her lawyer was H. Carpenter, a noted constitutional lawyer. The written decision by the judges included this passage "that God designed the sexes to occupy different spheres of action and that it belonged to men to make, apply and execute the laws was regarded as an almost axiomatic truth. . .A direct participation in the affairs of government, in even the most elementary form, namely, the right of suffrage was not then claimed, and has not yet been conceded. . .In view of these facts that when the Legislature gave to this court the power of granting to practice law, it was not with the slightest expectation that this privilege would be extended equally to men and women. Application is denied"[27]

Another judge by the name J. Field had this to say, "man is or should be woman's protector and defend her the paramount and mission of woman is to fulfill the noble and benign office of wife and mother."[28] What if the woman is single asked Myra

---

[27] History of Woman's Suffrage, v. 2, p.611
[28] History of Woman's Suffrage, v.2, p. 605

and his retort was still that it was the natural law for a woman to be protected by man.

Myra Bradwell started the **Chicago Legal News,** a paper that became so prestigious that cases and legal information printed in it became accepted in court as legal evidence. Not only did this occur for the Illinois Supreme Court in Illinois, it also became true for the United States Supreme Court. Myra was admitted in 1890 to the bar in Illinois but it became effective with the original date of 1869 which made her the first woman lawyer admitted to the bar.

Women sued for the right to attend law school and practice but not many of them pursued the vocation. During World War II because so many men were fighting in the war and the colleges needed students, women were pursued as students and many did take advantage of the offer. When the war ended, however, the women did not continue as lawyers but returned to being at home. The next thrust of women pursuing law degrees was in the 1970's.

Louisa Alcott was born November 29, 1832 in Germantown, Pennsylvania. She was a writer of short stories, poems, and books but the book she is most noted for writing is Little Women in 1836. She also wrote Little Men in 1871 and Jo's Boys in 1886. She did not become rich with her writing as she was only paid $5 for <u>Little Women.</u> She worked against slavery and as a Civil War nurse; she wrote a book of her experiences.

Even though she did not have much money, her friends shared what they had with everyone and Louisa knew Walt Emerson and was asked to visit him at Walden Pond which she frequently did. She socialized with Frederick Douglass and was involved with the abolitionist movement. She was one of the first ones to vote when Concord allowed women to vote in local elections and she went door to door urging people to vote and to work for suffrage. She never married but she did take of her niece after her mother died. She died March 6, 1888.

Julia Ward Howe, born May 27, 1819 was a poet known for the "Battle Hymn of the Republic." Her father was well-off and as a young child, she wished to be a writer. Her father did not consider that an appropriate profession. At age 22, she married Samuel Gridley Howe, an educator of the blind. His philosophy was that a woman remained at home almost in isolation, known as the woman's sphere. A wife did not speak in public nor take part in causes. He was very domineering and expected Julia to obey. They had six children and Julia did what he expected helping with **The Atlantic**

Monthly which he started in 1862. She also helped publish **The Commonwealth**, an abolitionist paper.

After many years of this domination, Julia railed against this treatment and they argued frequently. She loved him but his control and berating made her rebel especially when the money her father left her was squandered by Samuel. In retaliation, she joined the AWSA group which Lucy Stone started for suffrage partly because it allowed men in the organization. Julia had worked with Lucy and Henry Blackwell to publish The **Women's Journal** from 1870-1890.

Women were working all over the country for suffrage, especially in the west. In 1869, Wyoming became a state and granted suffrage to the women of the state. One of the main women who helped bring about that victory was Esther Morris. When Wyoming delegates went to Washington to get their state admitted to the union, they were told the women could not vote and their answer they would not enter without them. Wyoming women had the first voting privilege.

Esther had worked for suffrage in the state and got her husband and three sons to promise to vote for suffrage. The governor of the new state was so impressed with Esther that he appointed her justice of the peace in South Pass, Wyoming. She tried forty cases in her time and not one of those cases was ever appealed. Women were also jurors and the men considered them intelligent, careful, and worthy of being there.

Elizabeth Cady Stanton and Susan B. Anthony were the main leaders of the NWSA and work then began to concentrate in the west getting new states and getting suffrage for women. Susan B. Anthony and Elizabeth Cady Stanton would travel back and forth across the country to implement, encourage, and advise women in the west along with other women in the west including Emmeline Wells, Abigail Scott Duniway and Carrie Chapman Catt.

The two organizations continued their work for rights of women each in different ways. There were two organizations with differing goals and little communication although they knew what each was doing. It tended to slow the process.

One of the leading speakers for suffrage was Elizabeth Cady Stanton in 1869. Elizabeth traveled on the Lyceum Tour for at least ten years giving speeches as did Susan B. Anthony. It was an extremely hard experience spending eight to ten months each year travelling under long and tiring conditions. Both earned a good sum of money and Elizabeth did not have to depend upon money from her husband.

It's also the way she helped send all her seven children to college. Henry did not make enough as a lawyer and journalist to send them; Elizabeth helped pay their fees. She was the person who wanted divorce and incompatibility included in women's rights. After the birth of her last child, Stanton seems to have lived a life separate from Henry although they were never divorced; both traveled many months for their jobs.

With the passage of the 14th and 15th amendments, Susan Anthony made a good case for the 14th amendment giving women the right to vote. Across the country, 150 women attempted to vote in an election. On November 1, 1872 Susan Anthony and fourteen other women including her three sisters went to register in Rochester, New York. At first the inspectors were unsure what to do so they contacted a local lawyer by the name of John Van Voorhis for an opinion. He was in favor of suffrage; he told the poling judges to let them register which they did. On November 5, they voted and November 14, they were arrested for illegally voting. Henry Selden, ex lieutenant governor of New York and John Voorhies agreed to be their lawyers and bail was set at $500 which Anthony refused to pay. She was free but was indicted on January 24 and bail set at $1,000 which Henry Selden paid over the objections of Anthony.

She was free until the trial; she spent the time giving speeches in Monroe County where Rochester was located. It was expected that the trial would be there as that is where she voted. People gave unsolicited money to defray the costs of this trial- people like Gerrit Smith, Matilda Joslyn Gage, Thomas Wentworth Higginson, and other sympathetic parties. The latter was a member of the American Women Suffrage Association. This was the second group which had started after the Civil War. Yet here they are supporting Susan Anthony which proved the tie they still held for the cause of suffrage.

Susan B Anthony

Susan Anthony had not expected to be allowed to register as she was going to use the refusal to sue and take it to all the way to the Supreme Court. The second surprise was that she was arrested. The last surprise was that the trial was transferred on May 22 to Canandaigua, the next county, by Robert Crawley who would be the prosecutor. A man by the name of Ward Hunt had been appointed as associate Supreme Court justice and would be the judge for this case; there were supposed to be two, but Nathan Hall did not preside with Ward Hunt but sat in the audience with the ex-president Millard Fillmore. This was the first criminal case for Mr. Hunt.

Another point was that Susan Anthony was arrested in New York; this should have been a state jurisdiction, yet a federal judge came to prosecute. On June 17, 1873, her trial commenced, and a jury was selected and sworn in. She asked for a writ of habeas corpus which is the right to ask why you are being charged with the crime; it was denied. You are born with this liberty by the Constitution and it cannot be suspended. It is against the law but obviously the prosecutors ignored that fact. It was denied as it has been other times along with Susan Anthony. The trial continued. Robert Crowley was the prosecutor for the federal court; he along with Nathan Hall and Ward Hunt were all presidential appointees by then President Ulysses S. Grant. Her case was listed as the United States vs. Susan B. Anthony not New York vs. Anthony.

Robert Crowley used the case of Minor vs. Happersett in 1873 as a basis of his prosecution. This case where a woman by the name of Virginia Minor in Missouri had done the same thing as Susan Anthony. She attempted to register and was refused; she went to court and sued. She went to the state circuit court first where the decision was against her and then the case went to the Supreme Court in the case of Minor versus Happersett; her husband was her lawyer. Chief Justice Waite gave these remarks, "the national Constitution does not define the privileges and immunities of citizens. The United States has no citizens of its own creation. The Constitution does not confer the right of suffrage upon anyone, but the franchise must be requested by the states."[29] The decision was that states are not required to allow women the right to vote.

Virginia Minor continued the protest of women's rights by refusing to pay her taxes August 26, 1879 saying it was taxation without representation. In 1881 she was on the legislative committee for constitutional amendments in her

---

[29] Suffrage and Politics, p. 5

state of Missouri. She introduced a petition for enfranchisement of women.

Henry R. Selden used the 14th amendment as his defense saying it protected citizens and Susan Anthony was one; Susan asked Henry Selden to allow her to speak and was not allowed to do that. According to law, you have the right to have witnesses and to hear testimony of those against you about your crime. Susan Anthony was denied this right too!

When both sides were finished, Judge Hunt then brought out a written paper in which he directed the jury to deliver a guilty vote; the jury was not allowed to deliberate or vote. Henry Selden objected and asked the jury to be polled which Judge Hunt denied. He then proclaimed Anthony guilty and fined her $100 for court costs. He asked her if she had anything to say and her comment was, "May it please your honor, I shall never pay a dollar of your unjust penalty. All the stock in trade I possess is a $10,000 debt incurred by publishing my paper **The Revolution,** four years ago, the sole object of which was to educate all women to do precisely as I have done, rebel against your man-made, unjust, unconstitutional forms of law that tax, fine, imprison and hang women, while they deny them the right of representation in the Government; and I shall work on with might and main to pay every dollar of that honest debt, but not a penny shall go this unjust claim. And I shall earnestly and persistently continue to urge all women to the practical recognition of the old revolutionary maxim, Resistance to Tyranny is obedience to God."[30]

Elizabeth Cady Stanton had this to say about the event, "One of the gravest services rendered by Miss Anthony to the suffrage cause was casting a vote in the 1872 presidential election in order to test the rights of women under the Fourteenth Amendment. For this offense the brave woman was arrested, on Thanksgiving Day. She asked for a writ of habeas corpus. The writ being flatly denied."[31] Stanton also tried to vote in an election but not arrested as was Anthony; her ballot was quietly removed. The verdict was delivered June 17, 1873. Ironically, it was less than a hundred years earlier that patriots fought at Bunker Hill against their oppressors.

And now the true focus of the arrest of Susan Anthony. It is 1873. The other ladies who had voted were not put on trial; Judge Hall said they would use Susan Anthony as a test case for all. Susan Anthony was a prolific speaker and well equipped to give insightful and accurate talks. She had become a model for the National Women's

---

[30] History of Woman's Suffrage, v. 2, p. 680
[31] Eighty Years and More, p. 180

Suffrage Association. She was targeted with a vindictive purpose.   She was not allowed the right to testify at her trial; the jury was not allowed to be polled, and she was given a guilty verdict without due process. It was determined that the actions were purely political with the goal of destroying Susan's creditability and that of the suffrage movement. Susan B. Anthony bore the brunt of the malicious hatred of the suffrage movement. She was maligned forty years in newspapers, cartoons, and defined as an evil woman even in political cartoons. Yet Susan made sure that the three men who allowed her to vote election day and were thrown in jail for allowing her to vote were vindicated and eventually pardoned by President Grant.

Susan B. Anthony gave a speech before Congress about her being arrested on April 3, 1873.

It was titled "Is it a Crime for U.S. Citizens to Vote" in Great speeches by Women. Here is a short quote, " Article 1 of the New York State Constitution says: No member of this state shall be disenfranchised or deprived of the right or privileges secured by any citizen thereof, unless by the law of the land or the judgment of his peers . . . laws may be passed excluding from the right of suffrage all persons who have been or may be convicted of bribery, larceny, or any infamous crime."[32] It was a

---

[32] Voices of Democracy, April 8, 1873, Oratory Prospect, "Is it a Crime"?

declaration that women are citizens and can vote and that she did not commit a crime by voting!

By this time, there were thousands working for the rights of women. The fight to defeat suffrage was going to continue even up to the last minute when the last vote for the last state to ratify the 19th amendment would be recorded on the books. By that time, Susan Anthony had passed on in 1906; her name was still used by adversaries in the southern states, in rejecting the 19th amendment, as the "most evil person in history." Cartoons usually showed her in a derogatory manner-as a spinster who was old, ugly, and hateful.

The largest organization started in 1874 was the American Temperance Union or CRTU with the president Annie Wittenmyer who served for five years when Frances Willard took over. She was for prison reform, labor laws, prohibition, and suffrage. The former president did not wish to help suffrage. People saw the problems with drunks both on the jobs and elsewhere. They were fighting to stop prohibition but felt that if it was passed, it could be repealed whereas if suffrage was passed, there would absolutely be no repeal, so they considered temperance the lesser of two evils. The Prohibition Amendment (18th) passed on January 16, 1919 which said the manufacture, transportation, and sale of liquor was illegal but not the consumption.

This is the only amendment that has been repealed and that was in 1933.

Both the temperance and suffrage organizations would face the strength of yet unknown forces that will block and defeat their efforts to pass laws for both. The Women's Christian Temperance Union would also slow the progress of the suffrage movement.

The suffrage forces abandoned the effort to attempt to use the courts (or the New Endeavor as it was called) to obtain suffrage after Susan B. Anthony had been arrested. They had worked tirelessly getting petitions sent to Congress, giving speeches, and helping to abolish slavery and getting the 13th, 14th, and the 15th amendments passed. From now they would go state by state working for suffrage and to the Congress of the United States to talk to the people of the states and the legislators of the states and federal government. Other women working for rights would pursue their own ways of protesting the inequality of women.

Two such ladies who did this were Abby and Julia Smith who lived in Glastonbury, Connecticut. They were from a wealthy family; the father had been educated at Yale and was a preacher. The mother knew French and Italian and was a good astronomer. Here is yet another woman who studied science and refuted the belief that women were not intelligent enough to absorb and apply the analytical subject matter of the sciences much less teach it to other women.

There had been five sisters all of whom had been educated at Emma Willard Seminary in Troy, New York. They all had unusual names. They were abolitionists but when slavery was abolished, they turned to suffrage. Haney Zephina tirelessly worked gathering signatures for the abolitionists; Cynthia Sacretia was a horticulturist. Laurilla Aleroyla taught art and French at Emma Willard's in Troy. They had knowledge of Hebrew, Greek, and Latin. Julia was the only woman to translate the Bible from Greek, Latin, and Hebrew which was published in 1876. She had done this to disprove a man who said the world was going to end in 1843 or1844. She translated it five times. She taught French and Euclidian Geometry at Emma Willard's. There's another woman knowing math so well that she teaches it; another disclaimer of the inferior woman not intelligent enough to comprehend. Look at the education these ladies had and what they did yet there was no recognition of their achievements.

They allowed William Lloyd Garrison to speak in their front yard when he was denied sites in Hartford, Connecticut. Their mother wrote an anti-slavery petition which she presented to congressman John Quincy Adams. They lived on a homestead in Glastonbury at Kimberly Mansion and were highly respected in the community; they lived on the old homestead and did their own work.

By the 1870's slavery had been abolished and there was only Julia and Abby left of the family being 81 and 76 years of age. They turned toward suffrage working for women and their rights which included their home of Kimberly Mansion. At this time their fight began with the tax collector, George C. Andrews. He raised their assessment a $100 along with two other widows but no men had been assessed higher taxes in the area. They learned how a widow paid $7,830 into the treasury but having no vote while six hundred men paid a total of $1,200 for all of them and many of them could not read or write.

The ladies refused to pay the higher assessment and the tax collector seized seven of their cows to pay the tax. The ladies refused to pay because they had no representation and it was sexual inequality. The ladies bought back four of the cows that had been seized and sold. More of the cows were seized and sold for taxes until there were only two left in 1876. Julia and Abby had named them Taxey and Votey. Four times their property was seized to pay their taxes. Fifteen acres of their land was seized illegally sold at auction for $78.35; this land was worth $2,000 and was sold before Julia and Abby could get to the auction. The delinquent taxes were only $50. The tax collector, Mr. Andrews, refused to allow them to speak in the community meeting. Julia proceeded to talk from a wagon outside the court. She was a great speaker, and this is considered one of her best and one of the top speeches in the country. Her speech ended up in a newspaper and was spread across the country giving publicity to their predicament. You can understand why they fought such injustice.

Now they could file suit against the tax collector for lack of due process of law. A defense fund was started in their name. Hair from cow's tails and flowers were made and sold at a Chicago bazaar. It was a long process, but the lawsuit was decided in Julia and Abby's favor in Hartford, Connecticut in1876.

The notoriety of their case brought much publicity for the suffrage movement. Newspapers followed the story carefully. This is what one source quoted, "The maids of Glastonbury planted themselves upon the right of the sex to suffrage. These two women deserve. . . .Other women have paid their taxes under protest but Abby and Julia have done more than protest; they have suffered loss, as well as inconvenience their property having been seized and sold again and again because of their honest conviction that taxation without representation was as unjust to women as to men."[33] Abby passed on but Julia married Judge Amos Parker who had helped sue for the confiscation of their property. They moved to New Haven, Connecticut where she passed on a year later.

Neither Julia nor Abby officially worked for suffrage but by their example and determination, they helped change history and bring recognition and help to what the suffragists were trying to do. Julia even spoke before legislative committees telling this story. She also spoke at the national convention of NWSA. There were many more of these women who in their small way were fighting just as hard to change what rights women could have even perhaps someone in your own family.

With the discovery of gold in California in 1848, masses of people surged out there to find the gold. Lands were opened for settlement. The women moved west with their families and unhindered by the restraints of the east began to experience and practice the freedoms they so desired. They were doing more than their share and thus demanded these freedoms.

One of these new women suffragists from the west was Carrie Chapman Catt. She was born on January 9, 1859 in Ripon, Wisconsin. But she

---

[33] History of Woman Suffrage, v.3 p. 329

moved to Charles City, Iowa with her family when she was seven and went to a one - room schoolhouse. All her life she was fascinated with living things- reptiles, insects, butterflies, lizards and snakes. Her father allowed her to bring examples home to watch and study until she brought home rattlesnake eggs. Her father immediately destroyed them, and she was not allowed the freedom of having items in the home ever again. She again proved that women did have the intelligence and interest to deal with science. She was always a very organized person and read a lot including Darwin's, The Origin of Species even though she did say there were things she did not understand. She rode to high school on a horse and applied herself in getting good grades.

When she graduated, she decided to go to college and asked her father if he would help her. He was a farmer, but he gave her $25 and told her she had to earn the rest which she did just as Lucy Stone and others had worked their way through college. She attended Iowa State. College cost about $150 a year. She taught school for $26 a month, washed dishes for $.09 an hour and worked in the library for $.10 an hour.

In college, she started a woman's drill team using broom sticks for guns. This was in operation till it was replaced by Physical Education. In her

second year of college, she also won the right to
speak in the Crescent Library Society. Women were
allowed to write essays about many topics but were
not allowed to read them in public so someone else
did the reading. She insisted that she be allowed
and achieved the honor of doing it. She also
became a public speaker in which one of her
speeches was explaining why women should have
the right to an education with this statement "how is
it possible that a woman is unfit to vote would be the
mother of a man who is?"[34]

In 1880 she graduated in three years being
the only woman in her class. She became a teacher
in Mason City, Iowa where she taught for three
years until she became the superintendent of the
schools. In 1885 she resigned from that job when
she married Leo Chapman who was a journalist
there and ran a newspaper. Married women did not
work so she worked with him in writing articles for
the paper **Women's World** including articles on
suffrage. For better opportunities, they moved to
California but unfortunately, Leo died of typhoid and
they lost everything.

She moved to San Francisco to live with her
aunt and earn a living. She continued writing and
became the first woman reporter. She worked by
writing articles for print, but she had to struggle with

[34] Wikipedia, Catt p. 26

male workers there who thought she would welcome their advances. I think we now call that sexual harassment but there were no laws to protect women from such treatment from men.

While there she met George Catt, an architect who built bridges; he had been a student at Iowa State also. He encouraged her to speak publicly on topics of current interest including immigration, abolition, and suffrage. She prepared speeches covering these three topics and others and gave speeches throughout the state.

In 1887 Carrie Chapman Catt moved back to Charles City to take care of her younger brother Will who was not well. She also went to the Iowa suffrage convention in 1889 where she was made secretary, lecturer, and organizer. In one year of traveling in Iowa, she helped form ten suffrage organizations.

In 1890 she attended the National Woman's Convention in Washington and gave her "Symbol of Liberty" speech that impressed Elizabeth Cady Stanton, Susan Anthony, Lucy Stone Blackwell and others. This was also the year when AWSA and NWSA had merged to become the NWASA. It had taken three years to accomplish this.

She also married George Catt secretly in 1890 and went on a speaking tour of the Northwest.

Other suffragists were angry that she married as they thought she would give up working for suffrage, but Carrie explained that George and she were a team and he was also a reformer. He told her he would earn the money and she would speak for suffrage so that's what they did; she was to spend part of the year working for suffrage. He also made sure that she had financial security; she received most of his assets which made her wealthy.

She traveled to South Dakota where she spoke to women and was impressed with the farm women but found that there was fraud in the election. The German and Russian immigrants could not read so others marked the ballot for them, or they printed two ballots each in different colors with the suffrage information and one without and these ballots were counted as no. There was no victory for suffrage. Carrie Chapman Catt also went to Kansas to speak and work for suffrage then being too tired to continue, she went home to Seattle to rest. She was supposed to go the national convention of NASWA to speak but came down with typhoid.

George's business moved to the east in Boston. They were close to Lucy Stone Blackwell, Henry Blackwell, and their daughter, Alice. Unable to do the work, Lucy had trained her daughter to be editor of the **Woman's Journal**. Now the suffrage movement is seeing a second generation of women in the field. Alice was also partly responsible in helping to get the NWSA and AWSA back together into one organization NAWSA along with Anna Howard Shaw and Abigail Scott Duniway.

One of these newer ladies in the movement was Emily Collins, who like the others saw the wrongs of not allowing women to vote. She wrote "I pined for that freedom of thought and action that was then denied to all womankind. I revolted in spirit against the customs of society and the laws of the state that crushed any aspirations and debarred me from the pursuit of almost every object worthy of an intelligent, rational mind. . .I read, with intense interest everything that indicated an awakening of public or private thought to the idea that woman did not occupy her rightful position in the organization of society; and, when I found the lectures of Ernestine Rose and the writings of Margaret Fuller and found that other women entertained the same thoughts that had been seething in my own brain, and realized that I stood not alone, how my heart bounded with joy!"[35] These were the same sentiments that Elizabeth Stanton had stated in 1840 when talking to Lucretia Mott when they both attended the Anti-Slavery convention in London .

---

[35] Ladies of Seneca Falls, p. 823

In 1892 Elizabeth Stanton and Lucy Stone retired from NAWSA as they were not in good health. Susan Anthony at 73 took over as president and Carrie Chapman Catt helped her in this position and spoke to the Congressional committee about its lack of interest. Susan Anthony asked to address Congress for support of the suffrage amendment. Aaron Sargent, a California representative, had met Anthony on a train out west and was impressed with Anthony so he introduced the amendment to Congress in 1878 and though rejected, it was brought up consistently.

Carrie Chapman Catt welcomed the opportunity to perform this deed. In 1893 she attended the Columbian Exposition where there was a display by the suffrage movement and speeches given by all the major leaders in the country. She noticed that the cartoons in the paper showed the suffragists coming from mental institutions while the anti-suffragists were pretty and dressed fashionably.

Carrie Chapman Catt was disturbed about actions of Elizabeth Stanton who had written a book called The Woman's Bible where she criticized and challenged the rhetoric of the Bible. Catt strongly felt the more traditional members would be insulted and drop membership and support. Elizabeth Cady Stanton was too radical in her actions even at Seneca Falls where she had urged a vote on divorce and incompatibility. She was the only one for years who lobbied for these two items to be part of the law. The members wanted to pass a resolution denouncing this action to get Stanton to drop the publishing. Carrie Chapman Catt and Susan Anthony had discussed the situation with Elizabeth Stanton, but she refused to drop her action. The organization did pass the resolution 54-41.

Although Susan Anthony had talked with Stanton about this bible she was writing, she still supported her and did not condemn. She suggested to the head of NAWSA that they not pass the condemnation which was ignored. It was the support that women should have for each other even if they do not agree and these two women had been comrades for many years.

Elizabeth Stanton wanted Susan Anthony and herself to sever their relationship with NAWSA. Susan remained loyal to Elizabeth Stanton but there was a distance between them and neither one of them left. Elizabeth Stanton wanted to pursue other ideas and wrote many articles about her ideas. This reflected Stanton's viewpoint of marriage; she consistently talked and wrote articles about marriage and divorce, dignity, personal freedom, full equality in marriage and even suggested using contraception. She was considered more radical and intellectual but in great demand as a writer rather than being ostracized.

After Elizabeth Cady Stanton retired as head of NAWSA, the New York Suffrage League council held a luncheon for her to honor her achievements. She was now called the "Grand Old Lady."

Susan Anthony arranged a party for her 80th birthday in November 1895 sponsored by the National Council of Women made up of twenty-two organizations. Six thousand people were in attendance along with thousands of letters and telegrams to celebrate her efforts for suffrage. This she wrote in her diary, "I thought of the Seneca Falls days. Who would believe then that in less than half a century, I at that moment the laughing-stock of the press and public. . . would to-day receive such a tribute?"[36]

It became harder and harder for her to manage outings even though she kept writing to the end. Two weeks before she passed away in 1902, she had written an article on divorce and one week before a letter to Theodore Roosevelt urging his support on suffrage.

In September of 1893, Carrie Chapman Catt was asked to go to Colorado and work on getting suffrage voted as part of the state constitution. She

[36] Eighty Years and More, p. 292

had to raise money and travel over the state speaking and opening fifty suffrage clubs. She traveled over 1,000 miles and the travel was difficult and the hours long. She went from place to place speaking early and late in the evening. Sometimes she took a train and one time there was a wreck and a man on a hand car came to get her and take her to her destination. By this time, it was 9 P.M. but the people were still there waiting for her. She gave her speech, caught a few hours of sleep and left at 4 A.M. for her next destination. These actions were mostly typical of most volunteers working for suffrage. Fortunately, Colorado voted in woman suffrage this time.

Carrie Chapman Catt went to work in New York with a great anti-movement against them saying that if suffrage was voted in, the people would also have prohibition. Catt gave over forty speeches to persuade the voters. The propaganda against suffrage was that women didn't really want the vote anyway and the Bible proved them to be the weaker sex.

Even though the suffrage women brought petitions to the legislators totaling 600,000, they were rejected while the 15,000 brought by the anti-suffragists were welcomed; needless to say, the suffrage vote failed.

Then it was to Kansas again to petition, visit legislators and talk to get their support, writing, and traveling to 103 counties of 104. The vote resulted in the same outcome as had become common to the suffragists-failure at the polls.

Carrie Chapman Catt went with Susan Anthony, who was unable now to do it all by herself to the southern states Kentucky, Alabama, Louisiana, and Tennessee in 1895. Anthony was by this time 75 years old and president of NASWA and still pushing herself speaking and writing. They had little success, but their mission was to push onward till the goal of an amendment to the Constitution was reached.

THE INVISIBLE ENEMY

Charging a Hat or Coat

In the forty years since the adoption of the 15th amendment, getting thousands of petitions with millions of names, raising money, traveling, and speaking, only seven states had secured referendums for women suffrage. Most were west of the Mississippi River except for Michigan (1874), Rhode Island (1887), and New Hampshire (1902). Those states in the west were Wyoming, Utah, Colorado, and Idaho.

It would be fourteen years more before any more states would approve suffrage. It was discouraging to all the women who had worked so hard. They wrote the letters, talked to the legislators who in many cases supported them in their efforts and promised to vote favorably. But when the time came for the election vote almost all of them voted against referendum proposals. This happened in too many states and the women questioned what had happened. As it occurred again and again, the "invisible enemy" so named in the book Suffrage and Politics thrust its head at their efforts all the time. They were not sure what it was, but they knew it was very powerful.

The epiphany came when delegates in each of the states that had rejected suffrage sent a report to National repeating the same stories over and over so that they knew it was not an isolated occurrence or a fluke; it was an organized plan of action carried out in many places. What did they learn? One big point stood out; there was voting fraud occurring in these elections. It was the mobilization of the foreign vote where illiterates were being paid to vote against suffrage-Germans in Nebraska, Missouri, and Indiana and in Oregon the Germans, Russians, the Chinese in California, and even the black freemen. The invisible enemy were men who buy and sell votes to sway an election in their favor. They built organizations of foreign-born populations to join in propaganda to force politicians to submit to their viewpoints. These men would be gangs that would bring the foreign born to the election and either read the ballot to them or they would have separate ballots that left off the suffrage question but the ballot would be read to them and they wrote an X and they would be paid for their vote and the ballot would still be counted as a no ballot. There were also more votes counted in the elections than there were people in the district meaning there was collusion with the election officials. Who was paying for all these votes? Today I believe this is called "ballot harvesting"

In 1881 the Brewer's Association clearly favored prohibition saying it could be repealed while suffrage was permanent. President Ruppert of the Brewer's Association denied this in 1918 while being investigated by the Judiciary committee. There were no records just the demonstration of what they did. In this case their actions spoke louder than any words.

The "Invisible Enemy" they found out was the liquor interests. In 1862 the Brewers Association was organized as a protection of the trade. This machine was made up of three organizations. They were the U.S. Brewers Association, the Wholesale Distillers Association, and the Retail Dealers Association. In 1867 the association made it very clear to both political parties that they would declare war on all candidates who favorably supported the agendas of the temperance or suffrage movements. It was the determination of this organization to implement the organizations of foreign born to defeat both movements at the polling places. The person who was responsible for organizing the tactics to be used in prohibition and suffrage campaigns was the same in both cases and reported to the boss their achievements in this matter.

Where did the liquor association get the money? It was raised by dues comprising of a half cent to a cent on each barrel of liquor. There was an equal amount of money from national and the state and if more money was needed, there would be another assessment. The money would be put into the treasury and checks would be written to individuals, political campaigns, or groups as payment. Usually each state would assess its own amount and send off the money. They left NO or very few written records of their business. Each month after the checks were written and returned along with the check stubs, everything would be destroyed. The man under contract paid by the liquor association $40,000 a year to organize and coordinate the sabotage of these campaigns was Percy Andreae. That amount of money is worth today to around $1,100,000.

The women who were working on suffrage campaigns began to realize what was happening and see the signs, but they could not prove it. They were frustrated and discouraged to the point of despair. They realized this was no ordinary policy of a campaign but a monster political machine hiding behind the deep secrets of intimidation and bribery. Women were sent out in teams to gather information and observe the events to see if they could identify the culprits. They wrote affidavits of what was occurring at these elections and sent it back to national. How interesting that almost all the reports contained the same or very similar accounts. Time after time in many of the states the suffrage amendment was defeated.

SUFFRAGE IN THE PACIFIC STATES

Charging a Hat or Coat

One of those states that kept failing to gain suffrage was Oregon; it took six attempts. The woman that worked tirelessly for suffrage in the far west was Abigail Scott Duniway. I am going to take you through her entire life to show the concentration and dedication she used to get suffrage in Oregon in 1912. She had already achieved suffrage in Washington and Idaho. The time and effort she put into the suffrage movement was a model of what other women did during the movement.

She was born in Groveland, Illinois October 22, 1834, one of twelve children. Abigail's father had signed notes for his brother Lindsey who gambled the money away and was killed by an angry mob. Her father moved the family to Wesley, Illinois where he bought a circular sawmill with a partner. He became very prosperous, but he got the western fever and decided to take the family to Oregon. He sold everything and started West for a new life.

Abigail and her family made the journey to Oregon in 1852; Abigail was seventeen years old. She took the Webster's Elementary spelling book with her to Oregon. She had only five months of schooling, but the family had many newspapers that she read thoroughly to improve her reading skills. She kept a diary of the journey which she used for information when she wrote <u>Captain Gray's Company</u>. She was fascinated by the new country and trails that she would wander off to explore as the wagons were moving west. She climbed the rocks and observed all around her getting so absorbed that she had to run to catch up with the wagons. Her father never said anything to the others where she had gone trying to teach her a lesson about staying with the group.

On the way, she lost her mother and a brother to what they thought was cholera. A young man, John McDonald, who had a crush on Abigail also drowned crossing a river. They arrived in Willamette Valley and her father opened a hotel, a Temperance House, and the girls of the family worked there but Abigail also was a self-taught teacher. There were visitors to the hotel also men who wished to be suitors to the girls.

Land grants were being given to men who married and helped settle the area. Eager suitors wanted to marry the girls to get the land. Ben Duniway had met Abigail when their family came to Oregon. They were married on August 1, 1853 and they moved out on a farm and built a home. She left out the word obey like Elizabeth Cady Stanton and Lucy Stone Blackwell in the wedding ceremony. By the end of 1853, they had a baby girl whom they named Clara. Abigail was busy doing the many chores and still many visitors stopped at the farms and people were very talkative so she would talk to them while doing chores. The women were also responsible for helping the sick and injured; they would visit and often told stories of their lives of the hardships and loneliness. Abigail recorded these in her diary and would use them later in her stories and speeches.

Ben was badly injured by a runaway team on the farm and was unable to do the farm work. He had also signed notes on the farm, and he was unable to pay them back when bad crops and weather destroyed them. Abigail had not signed the notes as women could not do that. Ben lost his land for the debt and they had to find another way to make a living. The family moved into Lafayette where Ben went to work on odd jobs that he was able to find.

With his former injury, he was never able to do hard labor again. Abigail became the breadwinner and opened a private boarding school; it did not do well so they took in women boarders instead. Then they moved to Albany, Oregon where she tried teaching again along with opening a millinery store with a partner and they sold hats and notions. To get hats, Abigail went to Portland where she asked Jacob Mayer for 75 hats; he gave her 300 hats which she sold in a week and came back to get more and this time, he gave her 3,000 hats.

This business provided income for six years. Women would come to buy and then sit and chat about their frustrations and hardships. It was an old story about not having any rights to make decisions about the children or having any money. They also talked of the abuse both verbally and physically. Sometimes Abigail would loan them money knowing she probably would not get it back. She also had two more sons while living here.

In 1870 the Duniway family moved to Portland. Abigail joined the active equal women's rights group. This group eventually evolved into the Oregon State Equal Suffrage Association and Abigail was a president for many years.

In Portland they purchased a printing press and opened a newspaper called the **New Northwest**. Abigail used her writing skills for suffrage and started lecturing. The children helped with the newspaper as there were now six of them, Clara being the oldest. Her son's names were Willis, Hubert, Wilkie, Clyde, and Ralph. Clara would care for the younger children while her mother did other work. Ben helped with the business affairs and the sons would help with the printing. It was indeed a "family" affair.

Abigail used her book that she had written in 1859, Captain Grays Journey and published it in serial form; the name was changed in 1905 to From the West to the West. She also wrote other books and published them in serial form. She wrote and published articles about women and suffrage and the struggles they had endured who had no recourse in gaining their rights. A lot of articles dealt with suffrage and slavery but not temperance. As I mentioned before the Women's Christian Temperance Union (WCTU) had more members than the suffrage and were also very antagonistic toward their efforts and were inhibiting the suffrage movement.

While in Portland, Abigail decided to have a suffrage lecture. They rented a hall Oro Fino because all the churches refused them permission to use their buildings. Abigail had invited Elizabeth Cady Stanton and Susan Anthony to come and speak but only Anthony accepted the invitation. There was a printed program and Ben sold tickets for $.50 each and was the ticket taker at the door. Cartoons were printed of Anthony that showed her as cranky and having the features of a witch. The women adversaries of suffrage often used "unladylike "language that was almost lewd. But besides Susan Anthony speaking, she persuaded Abigail to speak and was well received. Both ladies were asked to speak at the Olympic Territory Legislature along with the anti-suffrage group.

Susan Anthony and Abigail Scott Duniway then spent two months traveling through Oregon, and Washington for suffrage; they traveled 2,400 miles. They rode trains, horses, coaches, buggies, and any conveyance they could find. They spoke in barns, saloons, stables, blacksmith shops even in an unfinished hotel where the floor collapsed as they were talking. Abigail known for her wit and calmness urged the audience to stay and listen which they did. Often, she included songs with her speeches that she had also composed; they were written with the popular tunes of the day. Her daughter, Clara, would sing the song.

They stayed in any lodgings that they could find so it is obvious that their journey was a hardship on them physically. The anti-suffrage forces followed them to the same place to harass and dispute their speeches. But they continued their journey. They also started the Washington Suffrage Association.

One-time Abigail was returning home on a stagecoach and one of the male passengers who was slightly inebriated and against suffrage said to her, "Madam, you ought to be at home enjoying yourself like my wife is doing. I want to bear all the hardship of life myself and let her sit by the fire toasting her footsies." The stage stopped and let the man off at his house. Abigail looked out and saw the wife chopping wood. She, leaning out said "I see, my friend, that your wife is toasting her footsies" Goodbye."[37] After that the man gained the nickname "Footsie Toaster."

Abigail Scott Duniway

At one time, her sons Willie and Hubert were arrested for assault and battery when they attacked a reporter. The story was that both had discovered an article in a newspaper of Abigail that was very

---

[37] Ladies Were Not Expected, p. 86

derogatory to the point of slander. They went to see the person and attacked him. They were put in jail and bail was set at $10,000. They would not tell their mother what it was but by the hesitation, it was surmised that it was vulgar and disgusting. Even the prosecuting attorney told them that they had done the right thing in defending their mother's honor.

Susan Anthony invited Abigail Duniway to come to the next national suffrage meeting in New York and speak. So, Abigail went traveling around 3,000 miles across the country and spoke before all the delegates of NWSA; it was May,1872, the same year Susan B. Anthony had voted and been arrested. Abigail was well received at national. Abigail felt that grassroots action would not help the suffrage cause. Instead she stressed good speaking and the support and information from the national cause would help most. She also believed that non-confrontational tactics and persuasion would work better with their rivals. Her beliefs would cause the younger suffrage women to disagree. There were many minds in the suffrage group and disagreement among the women would cause eruptions, discussion, and compromise. As a result of attending this national convention, Abigail was made one of five Vice-Presidents-at-large.

Abigail Duniway, Maria Handee, Mrs. M.A. Gambert, and Mrs. Beatty, an African American, voted in the presidential election joining Susan Anthony and Francis Minor in the voting. In the case of the first four, their ballots were taken by the election judge and placed under the ballot box. They were not counted but it set a precedent and harbinger of the suffrage movement. The latter two were arrested and had court trials but only Francis Minor had a Supreme Court hearing and decision.

In 1887, Ben became ill; Abigail went home to help; Ben did not recover, and his illness kept him incapacitated. He passed away in 1896. They decided to sell the paper and Abigail would spend the next seven years working for suffrage in Oregon, Idaho, and Washington. She had also helped, along with Lucy Stone in 1890 helped the two groups of NWSA and AWSA merged into NAWSA.

She also had another weekly newspaper called **Pacific Empire** which she ran from 1895-1897. This paper also addressed women's rights and the suffrage movement using many of her own writings. She was a prolific writer with over twenty-two novels most of them about women and suffrage. In 1914, she wrote Path _Breaking_ which was her autobiography.

She got suffrage for Idaho in 1896 and Washington in 1910; she was even asked to write the suffrage documents for that purpose, but Oregon remained out of the column. The newer suffragists blamed Abigail and she blamed her brother, Harvey, who was head of the Oregonian and wrote numerous editorials against the suffrage cause. He had helped her a lot with their paper, but he did not support suffrage and wrote against it in his paper. They defeated suffrage in 1884, 1900, 1906,1908, and 1910 finally gaining it in 1912. Oregon had the most attempted number of times trying for suffrage-six. Only South Dakota took almost as many-five. The governor of Oregon, Oswald West, asked her to write the suffrage document. She was there when it was signed; the governor had seen and heard her speak when he was ten years old and was awed. She was also the first woman to vote in Oregon.

She wrote her autobiography Path Breaking in 1914. She passed away October 11, 1915.

Mary Olney Brown was a suffragist in the northwest territory and worked with Abigail Scott Duniway. In what is now Washington, a law was passed in 1867 basically saying that all white American citizens above the age of twenty-one had the right to vote. This legislation came from Edward Eldridge who deliberately left out the word male; he felt woman should vote. His intention was to give women the right to vote as he was a champion of woman suffrage. The wording was clear even though the men disputed the interpretation. Mary Brown urged all women to vote in 1869 but most were afraid of the consequences. Mary Brown did go to the polls and got her daughter to go with her. People said she would be insulted by trying as was the case since both their votes were rejected. In 1870 they tried again at various locations at Grand Mounds, Black River and Olympia. Mary's sister Charlotte Olney French took and group of women to vote also. Except for Mary's polling place, of the others they were allowed to vote in another precinct, but the votes were not counted, and the ballots were included in the total number of people voting. In the Olympia precinct the judges ruled the voting as illegal.

Then the 1871 legislative term wrote a law saying stating specifically that no female shall have the right of ballot or vote at any poll or election. Mary Brown, president of the suffrage association of Washington took petitions and canvassed women to sign for suffrage stating that women were for the most part ignorant of what was being offered. To inform women she wrote five articles on **Equality of Citizenship** and these were all published in Duniway's **New Northwest.** The legislature of

Washington passed the law that rescinded the right of women to vote but in 1910, suffrage came to Washington partly because the Brewer's Association was caught off guard.

There were quite a few men who supported women's rights, and this is a small example along with Abigail's husband, Ben, who worked along with women for suffrage. As men began to accept the right of women to vote, more men joined. After all it was still all men who passed the amendment in Congress and in the state legislatures.

I took Abigail Duniway through the whole process of suffrage to show a continuous line of work. Abigail worked forty years with suffrage devoting time and money. She was a forceful woman and did have confrontations with others but persisted in spite of it. She was considered a prominent force in getting suffrage in the pacific states. Her family worked tirelessly with her all the way. She learned long before some others that immigrants were voting illegally. There were German newspapers that were manipulating elections with a preponderance of stories that were total fabrications. (fake news) The immigrant groups that were voting or being brought to vote, in many cases could not read or write.

One more woman helped with suffrage in the west, in fact, with the state of Utah. Her name was

Emmeline Wells. She was born February 29, 1828 in Petersham, Massachusetts. She became interested in the Mormon church through her mother and joined the church in 1842. At the age of 16, she married James Harris, also a new member, and they moved to Nauvoo, Illinois, a thriving Mormon settlement. She had one son who died as an infant. James left one day in order to find work to support his family and while gone, he died. To earn money, she became a teacher and was teaching two children of Newell Whitney, a much older man whom she married; Mormons practiced plural marriages. In 1846 the extended family journeyed to Salt Lake City in the Utah territory and the center of the Mormon religion. They had two daughters. Newell also passed on in 1850. Left with two daughters to support, Emmeline went back to teaching and writing. She was noted for being a thinker and organizer.

Emmeline went to Daniel Wells who was a leader in the church and asked him to marry her. He already had six other wives and children but married her in 1852. They had three daughters along with her other two and Emmeline was mainly responsible for supporting them. Emmeline had started writing a journal in 1848 and continued them till about 1920 when she was ill. As I mentioned before, the journals are where so much knowledge of their thoughts and actions provide information about what the women did; she had forty-six journals by the time she passed away.

Emmeline became editor of the **Woman's Exponent**, a newspaper published twice a month. It had started in 1872 although Emmeline did not start then. She served in this post from 1877-1920. She wrote editorials of various topics including woman's rights and the right to vote and run for office. She used the name Blanche Beechwood for articles about suffrage. She worked for suffrage from 1879-1914. "I believe in women. I desire to do those things that would advance women in moral, and spiritual, as well as educational work."[38]

In 1879 Emmeline Wells was appointed to be Utah's representative to the National Suffrage meeting in Washington, D.C. by Susan Anthony and Elizabeth Cady Stanton who became her lifelong friends. Utah had suffrage but had it rescinded; it was Emmeline Wells who worked diligently to restore it and did in 1896. She worked with Congress to address issues especially the concept of plural marriages which she supported. She was president of the Utah Territorial Suffrage and even went to London to speak before the International Council of Women.

---

[38] A-Z Quotes, Wikipedia, Emmeline Wells

In 1876 Brigham Young had asked her to manage a grain saving program for the church which she did till World War I. In 1919 Woodrow Wilson paid her a personal visit to give her a commendation for selling wheat to the U.S. government when they needed it for the soldiers during the war.

At the age of 82 Emmeline accepted the presidency of the Mormon Relief Society where she served from 1910 to 192I when she passed away.

MAKING ONE SUFFRAGE GROUP - NEW LEADERS

Charging a Hat or Coat

The people in a democratic country are expected to be knowledgeable about what is occurring in their country. The rights of the people are protected and "due process" is the order of business yet the men still controlled this process and were usurping this power to eliminate people who stood in their way of what they wanted. We study history to learn what happened in the past and not repeat the mistakes that have occurred. In this scenario it was the right of women to vote. The women learned what was inhibiting their progress and kept petitioning members of Congress, talking to the public and raising money to fight. Donations may have come in by pennies, but the totals amounted to millions.

From 1895 to 1900 Carrie Chapman Catt was head of the organizational committee of NAWSA as she was a superb organizer. She raised money for the organization and opened suffrage groups in many states. Catt made a concerted effort to get more members in the suffrage movement; she used the Women Clubs for her target. These were upper class women seeking an outlet of performing charitable actions and reforms in the country. Catt never considered herself as leader of the suffrage movement; she left that role to Elizabeth Stanton and Susan Anthony. She was only an officer of NAWSA. In 1890 The two groups had merged together to form a more cohesive organization.

Susan Anthony had resigned as president; she was eighty by this time having been working for fifty years. She would spend the time working on yet another volume of <u>History of Woman Suffrage</u> with Ida Husted Harper and Elizabeth Cady Stanton who was now eighty-five.

In 1900 Carrie Chapman Catt was elected president of NAWSA. Her husband, George, had encouraged her to run for president. He had always supported her working for the suffrage movement and had made her sign an agreement when they were married that she would work for suffrage at least two months a year.

Anna Howard Shaw and Carrie Chapman Catt were the main candidates for office, but Susan Anthony had given her support to Carrie believing that she was the better candidate. Anna Shaw had more experience but not considered a good organizer and reacted when she did not approve of actions of other members which caused dissension and hard feelings.

Carrie Chapman Catt took over for her to publicize the suffrage movement; she brought back vitality and interest to the public notice. She encouraged them to have a fair of goods from each state in the Madison Square Garden. There were figs and pecans from Georgia, sugarcane and molasses, citrus fruits from Florida, flour and butter from Kansas, pigs from Iowa, native American artifacts from the western states, and much more. The result of this undertaking brought in $10,000 to the NAWSA treasury.

Carrie Chapman Catt

In 1903, Carrie Chapman Catt traveled with her husband to Italy, France, Switzerland. Catt had organized and started the International Women's Suffrage Alliance in 1902 which she was supporting.

Returning to the U.S. Catt and her husband moved into Manhattan selling their house. As

George had not fared well on the trip, they felt the need to downsize. Because of this, Catt decided not to run for president in 1904 but stay home and take care of George and to open the International Woman Suffrage. Anna Howard Shaw was elected president with Carrie Catt as vice-president. For over a year, Catt nursed him, but he died in October,1905, and unfortunately, she lost interest in the suffrage movement. He had supported her through all the years with the suffrage movement being a reformer himself; he believed strongly in what she had done.

Carrie Chapman Catt was left grief stricken but a very wealthy widow. She could not even live in the apartment where they had lived so she moved in with a friend, Mary Hayes. They lived together till Mary died. In 1907 Catt lost both her mother and brother, Will. It was an overwhelming loss and she needed time to grieve. In 1910, she had an operation and was told to rest for a year and in 1911, she took a 76 - day trip to Sweden and India where she met Mohandas Gandhi who would be the guiding force of revolution for independence of India.

Coming back, she again entered the suffrage movement increasing the membership to 100,000 and driving the members to push for a suffrage amendment. Over this long of a time, these new members were of a different resolve and that was one of more radical actions including picketing and physical confrontation.

The leader of this new force was Alice Paul, also a Quaker. Alice Paul was born January 11, 1885 in Moorestown, New Jersey. By the date you can tell the distance of ages between the suffrage leaders. There was a gap of seventy years between Elizabeth Stanton and Alice Paul and around twenty-six between Carrie Chapman Catt and Alice Paul. Paul's history was involved with temperance but mostly with suffrage. Her mother would take her to these suffrage meetings as a child; she was weaned on the belief that suffrage was important.

She had a very impressive family tree; her mother was descended from William Penn and her father from John Winthrop of Massachusetts. The original Pauls left England for religious freedom. Her father was a successful businessman of profitable real estate and they lived on a farm. Her father died when she was sixteen and her uncle, Don Paul, managed her finances.

Alice attended Swarthmore College which Lucretia Mott had helped to establish. She played tennis and sports and one of her good friends was Mabel Vernon who would also be a co-worker and creator of the National Working Party with Alice. She did so well in her course work that she was awarded an associate fellowship in New York by a professor. She received a BA in Biology at Swarthmore in 1905 and a Master of Arts (MA) in Sociology at what is now Columbia University in 1907. She also received a PhD. in 1912 after returning from England at Western Pennsylvania.

After graduation, Alice went to London where she met some of the more radical suffrage workers including Mrs. Emmeline Pankhurst who was British and Lucy Burns who was American. Emmeline Pankhurst was head of the WSPU (Women's Social and Political Union). Only women were allowed in the organization. They were concentrating on one priority (suffrage) and did not work with other groups. In politics they protested all candidates in the government in power. Their strategies were hunger strikes, picketing and even violence-smashing windows, and spitting on officers. They were arrested numerous times. Alice met a group of them in a police station where they had been arrested; there were fifteen of them. What was interesting was that twelve of them had attended or graduated from college. Ten of them had been married at least once, five were divorced, and even had children. Their vocations included law, historians, actresses, nurses, or architects. These new suffragists were well educated as the early ladies had fought and won the right to have education.

Alice returned to the United States in 1910 to join NAWSA where she quickly began voicing her opinions-the biggest being that there should be concentrated efforts to secure a national suffrage amendment. NAWSA, at this time, was only interested in getting a suffrage amendment through state legislatures. Alice was appointed to be the head of the Congressional Committee and Lucy Burns worked with her as they had both been together in London with Emmeline Pankhurst. NAWSA believed the organization needed new ideas and action and Alice was felt to be able to do this.

Alice Paul

This committee was originally headed by Alice Kent, the wife of a congressman. Her budget was $10, and even that was seldom used. The Congressional Committee was a standing committee which was supposed to reach out to committees of Congress addressing concerns how to achieve suffrage. Alice Paul felt lobbying was the key in getting an amendment and in 1912 persuaded NAWSA on this point. Alice Paul started an auxiliary committee under the Congressional Committee called the Congressional Union. Its purpose was to raise money for the purpose of demonstrations, parades, or activities to arouse the awareness of suffrage.

National was in favor of this new idea but stated specifically that the committee had to raise their own money. Alice Paul had witnessed what Emmeline Pankhurst had done in England and felt this method would be more effective. What Paul did here is basically what Pankhurst had done in England. She first followed a simpler version to work with NAWSA; she was strong willed and had definite ideas to implement.

Alice Paul wanted to have a national parade in order to focus interest on suffrage particularly on a federal amendment to the Constitution. Alice Paul said, "When you put your hand to the plow, you can't put it down until you get to the end of the row"[39].

Her goal was a federal amendment not anything else not birth control, divorce, or abortion. After achieving that, the next level was to secure equal rights and remove legal inequalities for all women.

Alice Paul was a charismatic motivator and speaker and her followers usually did what she wanted; she was aware of the power she had and what she could get them to do. A big problem was that other members of NAWSA opposed her actions feeling she was too militant with her ideas that she wished to implement. National was aware of the militant actions carried out in England and predicted it would come to the U.S. and it was now here.

Carrie Chapman Catt and Anna Howard Shaw both had conflicts with Alice Paul over strategy and theory. The national did not want the tactic of blaming the party in power for not having suffrage or working against candidates just because they were in that party, the "party responsible". This is what England had done and Paul brought these ideas home. Some Democrats were for suffrage. What was also different in England was that there was only one party in power. The Prime Minister and all the members of Parliament were all from one party. Whereas in the United States the President could be one party with members of the Congress from both parties.

---

[39] From Equal Suffrage to Equal Rights, p. 96

Carrie Chapman Catt used diplomacy and compromise to keep Woodrow Wilson on her side while Alice Paul blamed the Democrats and Wilson as their leader. Carrie Chapman Catt did not confront Woodrow Wilson with the suffrage question but kept introducing the ideas to him privately. There were both Democrats and Republicans who supported suffrage and those who opposed it. Carrie Chapman's Catt's agenda was to keep them talking and pushing suffrage. When you're trying to reach a goal, it is unwise to alienate any who have the power and resources to help you get to the conclusion. A discussion of both viewpoints is essential along with compromise.

Very obviously these were not good working conditions. In studying these women of history, this is one characteristic of most of them who achieved their goals was to have patience and understand what others thought even though they may disagree and work with that point trying to change their minds. There was disagreement among them, sometimes very vocal but not vicious or stories that were not true. There was civility and compromise.

When Alice Paul wanted to have a suffrage parade, NAWSA supported the idea wholeheartedly. The Congressional Union had to raise the money themselves and met the challenge raising $27,378. The problem that occurred was that the money was not sent to the national treasury as was usually the rule with money raised or donated. The CU kept the money in a separate account which brought suspicion against Alice Paul and her committee. The incident and what happened to the money was carefully checked along with an audit. It was found that there was no wrong- doing and every penny was accurate and accounted for in the audit.

The national members cooperated and assisted in the efforts to get the floats and organization going. The parade was planned for March 3 because that was when Woodrow Wilson would be coming to Washington, D.C. for his inauguration; they thought it would a very evident show of the absence of followers waiting to see him when they were at a parade.

Woodrow Wilson

The parade was held on March 3, 1913. Paul had asked for a permit for the parade route up Pennsylvania Avenue to the White House which was where Woodrow Wilson would be inaugurated. In case anyone is wondering, the inauguration date had not yet changed to January 20. The Constitution had set March as the date so the preceding presidents would have time to move out.

The police at first refused their permit due to the unsuitable conditions. Other women used their political and family connections to get permission. As the police were concerned about losing their funding, they granted the right to conduct a march on that date. The logistics of the parade were well planned with beautiful floats, bands, and thousands of marchers.

The one thing that wasn't thought out was the placement of the African American suffragists and Paul suggested they not march at all so as not to alienate the southern suffragists. NAWSA had promised all could march. The southern delegation did not like but this was the best choice. NAWSA decided they should march at the rear except for Ida Wells Barnett who told them, she would only march with the Illinois delegation and went to the sidelines then quietly slipped in to march with the Illinois people.

Ida Wells Barnett was born into slavery on July 16, 1862. She was a noted journalist, abolitionist and feminist who led an anti-lynching campaign in the 1890's. She met Ferdinand Barnett who was a journalist and active in civil rights in Chicago and married him.

Ida Wells Barnett

Ida Wells Barnett, Margaret Murray Washington, Frances Harper, and Harriet Tubman also started the National Association for the Advancement of Colored Women; Mary Church Terrell was its first president. Because of her efforts along with Jane Adams, a very needed housing project was built in Chicago in 1913. The same year she formed the Alpha Suffrage Club which was the first and most important African suffrage club.

Getting the southern delegates to join NAWSA was a tricky situation so by putting the African Americans at the back was a conciliatory response along with not allowing them at the national conventions. This was their compromise in this situation.   It was not handled well and did not really settle the problem.

Inez Milholland

At the very beginning of the parade was Inez Milholland who was young and pretty on a white horse in a white cape. They intended to show the public that suffragists were not all old ugly spinsters as the press always pictured them in cartoons. Second in the parade were representatives from twenty or more countries that already allowed voting for women. Third were the suffrage pioneers who had worked so diligently for the movement - Lucretia Mott, Elizabeth Stanton and Susan B. Anthony were already gone. Then came the NAWSA state delegations of women. Behind them were the floats, bands, and supporters of suffrage.

Woodrow Wilson had arrived in town for his inauguration and wondered where all the people were that he had been expecting to greet him. He was told they were at the suffrage parade instead of greeting the new president.

At first the parade went well, as the workers had spent time and money to exhibit themselves. There were over 8,000 people in the parade and 500,000 bystanders. Then the crowd began hurling insults, and heckling. They gained momentum with taunting remarks, spitting, throwing rocks and cigar butts, and even going among the marchers pushing and mauling the marchers, slapping, and pinching the women.

The police chief Major Richard Sylvester had originally asked that the march be postponed or cancelled but the ladies had already spent their money on the advertisement thus refusing his suggestion. Very obviously the police had an aversion for doing their job and let men in the crowd grab the women and manhandle them. One policeman said to Genevieve Stone, the wife of a congressman, "If my wife were where you are, I'd break her head".[40] The result of this chaos was that ambulances were called to the scene and around 200 people had to be treated and 168 arrested. They had to call in the army to handle the out of control crowd.

There were congressmen and senators with their wives who were marching and after seeing the travesty demanded an investigation. Why didn't the police have more force to keep order? Why didn't the police protect the marchers? This is what the congressmen demanded from the police and due to all the evidence and witness accounts, the police chief was fired.

The march brought chaos and disorder because of the violence but it certainly did bring attention to the suffrage forces. Alice Paul was very satisfied with the outcome that so many women had marched and that the public began to realize that the women were serious about their cause of voting and equal rights. Even though there was violence, it did not seem to bother Paul as she saw the same thing from her experience in England; she felt it was achieving a goal. It did bother the other suffragists. At the national in December of 1913, the delegates heard firsthand details from representatives who had been at the parade.

---

[40] From Equal Suffrage to Equal Rights, p. 30

Between NAWSA and the Congressional Union, the tension was volatile. When national let them start the Congressional Union, it was hoped it would bring in new ideas and vitality to the movement. Each side was suspicious of the other. The NAWSA suffragists felt that perhaps the new CU was a little too militant while others wanted Alice Paul to compromise which is why they asked her to give up the CU or be replaced as a chair of the Congressional Committee.

Refusing this suggestion, there were now two committees with two different women. It also meant that both women were in contact with congressional committees operating separately with different ideas but having one goal of suffrage. In 1914 a member of NAWSA, Ruth Hanna McCormick announced that the group was going to support the Shaforth Amendment which was that suffrage would only be a state's right issue. She had acted entirely on her own and had not cleared it with national. Her father, Mark Hanna, had urged his daughter to do this. It put them in a precarious situation since that was not the intent of all members. It was defeated in Congress along with the idea of a suffrage committee thus settling the controversy, but it brought bad feelings.

Alice Paul and her committee had met with Woodrow Wilson on March 7 after the 1913 parade asking him for his support of a federal constitutional amendment, but he told them the time was not yet right. That was the same comment made to the suffragists after the Civil War. They also started **The Suffragist**, a newspaper to keep other women informed of their itinerary of their work. New members of the CU were Mabel Vernon, Doris Stevens, Lucy Burns, Inez Milholland, and others and here is the background of these suffragettes. The difference between suffragists and suffragettes was the use of militant and confrontational tactics which you will soon read of their exploits.

Woodrow Wilson

Mabel Vernon was another member of CU that had gone to Swarthmore with Alice Paul and they had become friends. She was born September 9, 1883 in Wilmington, Delaware. She graduated in

1906 and taught German and Latin at Penn High School; she also in 1924 got her MA in Political Science. She was one of the most militant suffragists. At President Wilson's address to Congress in December 1914, she and four others sat with a concealed banner. When he was talking, all of them stood and on the banner were these words "Mr. President, what will you do for Woman Suffrage". She traveled to Ohio, Colorado, Utah, and Washington to establish suffrage associations and see that conventions were held in 1915.

By 1916 it was clear that the new group of women were the antithesis of what NASWA was trying to establish. So, the two groups split and the WNP (Working National Party) evolved and Mabel became the secretary of this group; they were able to raise a considerable sum to fund their mission. And again, on July 6, 1916, Mabel interrupted President Wilson's speech D.C. by standing and saying, "Mr. President, if you sincerely desire to forward the interests of all people, why do you oppose the national enfranchisement of women?"[41]

Other women that stood with the WNP included Maria Montessori, Alva Belmont, a wealthy divorced socialite, Dorothy Day, Phoebe Hearst, Chrystal Eastman, and Harriet Stanton Blatch,

---

[41] Archives of Women's Political Communication, Iowa State University, Carrie Chapman Center for Women and Politics, Wikipedia

daughter of Elizabeth Cady Stanton along with others; NWP had around 2,000 members. They found women who would support the new group and gave pledges and urged other women to do the same. The young organizers already had educations from colleges like Vassar, New York University, and John Hopkins which had not existed in 1848. These women were seeking new ideas for getting suffrage.

This break caused double work because there were now two groups seeking appointments with congressmen. Depending on which group was first, the congressmen would be confused what the women expected of them. WNP was asking for the Congress to introduce a federal amendment to be added to the Constitution while NAWSA was still seeking suffrage through the states. Because the methods of the WNP were more militant, the anti-suffragists and the congressmen tended to use this point as a reason to refuse to consider the suffrage amendment.

Lucy Burns was born July 28, 1879 in Brooklyn, New York. She was Irish Catholic and went to Vassar and Yale and after graduating taught at Erasmus for a while. In 1906, she went to Germany to study languages and got another degree from Bonn in 1908 and then went to England where she joined the Women's Social and

Political Union. The women in other countries were after suffrage and started such organizations for the purpose of gaining the vote along with other rights. She learned militant methods and was imprisoned and jailed for her methods. There she met Emmeline Pankhurst and Alice Paul. Lucy Burns would receive the reputation of being the suffragette who was arrested the most times.

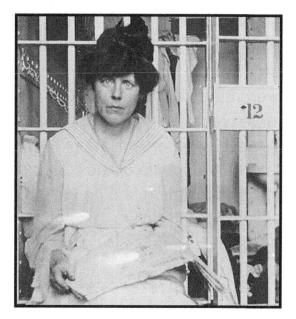

Lucy Burns

Lucy returned to the United States and joined NAWSA and was on the Congressional Committee with Alice Paul. Lucy Burns was the first woman to speak before congressional debates; Woodrow Wilson had told Lucy Burns he would support suffrage but went back on his word. Thereafter the CU would make the Democratic party responsible and worked on that premise and that women would unite as a voting bloc. CU sent two delegates each to nine states to get them to vote against democratic candidates but failed in their effort to defeat all democrats. In 1915 the CU was organizing branches in as many states as possible.

NAWSA was having internal strife, so Anna Howard Shaw resigned. Lucy Burns and Alice Paul met with the officers of NAWSA at Willard Hotel in D.C. to work out their differences and come to a compromise but there were only demands. The demands were that the CU not work against the Democratic party and blame them; they also wanted them to pay a fee to be an affiliate of NAWSA as they had established all the groups. In the end there was no reconciliation and so in 1916, the CU split from NAWSA and became a separate entity calling itself NWP or National Working Party.

Alice Paul was the president of this organization and Lucy Burns was the organizer, the one who was the orator and did the lobbying, writing, and was responsible for news bulletins much like what Susan Anthony did for NAWSA.

A third member of this new militant group was Doris Stevens born October 26, 1892. She went to college at Oberlin financing her education by teaching music as she was an accomplished piano and cello player. She graduated in 1911 where Lucy Stone had graduated in 1847. Doris settled in Greenwich Village noted for militant or bohemian people. In 1913 she and 500 other women were arrested and 168 were jailed but Doris only spent three days in jail and was given a pardon.

In 1914, she helped raise $50,000 for the CU and the NWP and then went to Colorado; In 1915 she went to California to the Panama Pacific Exposition. She served as personal assistant to Alva Belmont. In 1917, while picketing the White House, she was arrested with fifteen others; they called themselves the "Silent Sentinels". She was put in jail and force fed; she wrote a book about her experience which she called Jailed For Freedom. Doris Stevens was married twice-first to Dudley Field Malone who was her lawyer when she was arrested and her second husband was reporter Jonathon Mitchell, a **New York World** reporter.

One other person who was an active member of NWP and believed in militant tactics and held the political party was Inez Milholland. She was born August 6, 1886. She attended Vassar and attempted to have suffrage speeches on campus but was refused the privilege, so she held one off campus in a cemetery. For her action, she was suspended but did finish school and graduated in 1909.

Traveling to Europe, she enrolled in Oxford or tried to and was denied admission for the reason of her gender. Returning to New York, she enrolled in New York University and received her law degree there. She joined the law firm of Osborne, Lamb, and Garran.

Inez Milholland

She was in the suffrage parade in 1913 that went down Pennsylvania Avenue where she was dressed in white robes, had a red crown, and rode a white horse (Gray Dawn).

She was introduced to a Dutch man, Eugen Jan Boussevain, who imported coffee beans from Java. They were married July 15 and took Henry Ford's Peace Ship to Europe for a honeymoon.

Coming back in 1915, Inez became one of the leaders of NWP. She became an avid speaker and was in demand for her ability as an orator. Her schedule was so full that it was wearing herself out because she had pernicious anemia. She was warned by her doctor to slow down and rest, but she ignored the advice and continued her speaking schedule. As a result, she collapsed at the end of one of her speeches and died November 25, 1916; she was only thirty years old and it made her a martyr. She is also the first woman to have a memorial service in the U.S. Capitol.

Harriet Stanton Blatch was born January 20, 1856, the child of Elizabeth Cady Stanton and Daniel. She grew up in the suffrage movement with her mother. She even helped her mother with the series of the <u>History of Woman Suffrage books.</u>

She graduated from Vassar College in 1878 and married her husband. Four years later they went to live in England. In 1902 the family moved back to New York. She helped to revive the suffrage movement with the inclusion of women laborers who had been ignored by the other groups. The Equality League of Self-Supporting Women was formed. They held their meetings outside, held parades and got the legislature of New York to vote for a suffrage amendment. By 1917, New York was the first state in the East where women voted. When W.W.I broke out, she supported the effort and worked for the League of Nations when it started. She was also a member of the NWP; she died November 20, 1940.

The suffrage movement is now at a hard crossroads; there are two organizations again working towards the same goal and at odds or disagreement with how that is to be done. The two groups are now NAWSA and NWP. Both groups will be vying for attention in legislative committees and votes. Carrie Chapman Catt was back as president of NAWSA since Anna Howard Shaw had resigned because she was not able to accept the militancy of Alice Paul and the NWP even though they tried to pressure her to do so.

Anna Howard Shaw was born February 14, 1847 in Newcastle-upon-Tyne in England but moved to the United States when she was four years old. They lived on a frontier farm and her father apparently abandoned them and Anna had to take the responsibility of the family as her mother had a nervous breakdown and her brother was ill. At twelve years old she earned money as a frontier schoolteacher. After the Civil War Anna moved in with her sister and attended high school.

Becoming interested in the Methodist religion and wanting to preach, she attended Albion College a year later in 1875 at the School of Theology. She became a minister in 1880 ordained as one of the first Methodist ministers in the U.S. She also attended the Boston School of Medicine where she graduated with a degree in 1886. She was originally refused ordination by the Episcopal Church even though she had passed the test with a top exam score.

Her first interest was working in the Temperance organization and it was there she met Susan B. Anthony in 1887 who introduced her to the suffrage movement. Anna Shaw then proceeded to lecture for suffrage in the Massachusetts association and AWSA (American Women Suffrage Association). Anna was one of the ladies who worked with others to get AWSA to join with NWSA and become one organization. It took three years and the group was now known as NAWSA.

Once she became involved with NAWSA, her dedication turned there. When Susan Anthony decided to retire in 1900, Anna Shaw ran for president along with Carrie Chapman Catt, but

Susan Anthony supported Catt. When Catt resigned in 1904, Anna Shaw was given a second chance and was elected president and served for eleven years not having an easy term of office. It was felt that the president of the suffrage organization should have diplomatic, political, and administrative expertise which many felt Anna Shaw lacked; besides, she was noted for her temper. Shaw resigned after her eleven years when she refused to accept the militant actions of Alice Paul. Carrie Chapman Catt returned as president in 1916.

Anna Shaw continued working for suffrage becoming chair of the Women's Committee of the U.S. Council of National Defense for which she received the Distinguished Service medal being the first woman to achieve it. At the end of the World War I, President Howard Taft urged her to lecture for world peace and the League of Nations started by Woodrow Wilson. In 1919 she belonged to the National Council of Lynching. In 1915 her speech at Waco, Texas "The Fundamental Principle of a Republic" is now considered one of the top 100 speeches of the 20th century.

Anna Shaw worked hard for suffrage even urging women at her speeches to follow through and work for the goal. She lived in Moylan, Pennsylvania with Susan Anthony's niece, Lucy Anthony. She did not live to see the passage of the

19th amendment passing on July 2, 1919. Her achievements led her to be inducted in the National Women's Hall of Fame in 2000.

REVIEW OF WHAT HAS HAPPENED UP TO NOW

Charging a Hat or Coat

We are heading towards the last years of the suffrage campaign for voting rights so let's reiterate what has happened up to this point. The calendar started in 1848 with the Seneca Falls convention and the first woman's meeting.

This started the chain of events with other meetings and conventions occurring frequently in the first years drawing more and more women and even men who supported their efforts. Women who came from the Temperance and Abolitionist movement adopted the ideas of suffrage also wishing to abolish the abuses that were prevalent in all three movements. The Abolitionist and Suffrage movements tended to be the most closely allied and many women in suffrage were originally in the abolitionist groups.

Year after year national conventions were convened in various cities mostly in the east with a growing following from 1850-1860. There was also a growing tension in the country because of slavery and the abolitionists were getting impatient with more violence to rid the country of slavery. The suffragists had worked for both groups feeling that by working this way, they would be rewarded for their efforts by being given the right to vote. The Civil War broke out in 1860 so the conventions were put on hold, but their work continued.

The women worked hard with the loyalty league and getting the 13th, 14th, and the 15th amendments for freedom, citizenship, and voting passed. Particularly with the 14th and 15th amendments, the suffragists advocated replacing the word man with all sexes. At this point, the abolitionists dropped all support for suffrage movement saying to the effect they needed to wait as it was the negroes time not theirs yet not negro women just negro men. The ladies initiated the idea of a 16th amendment to get suffrage but that also did not happen but for years the 16th amendment became the model for suffrage until it became the Federal income tax.

The women had to expedite their next course of action and move forward; two groups formed each having different opinions so a division of these became NWSA (National Women Suffrage Association) with Elizabeth Stanton and Susan Anthony and AWSA (American Women Suffrage Association) with Lucy Stone Blackwell and her husband. With this arrangement there was no cohesive organization and resulted in duplication and expense but both groups held conventions and worked hard for suffrage.

After Susan Anthony was arrested in 1872 for voting, the tactic of using the courts (called New Endeavor) to get suffrage was abandoned and a new plan of action was created. It moved to getting states to vote in suffrage by using the legislatures and campaigns in the states one by one. The main target was the west. People were moving rapidly west to claim and developing lands for settlement and searching for gold and other minerals. The population grew exponentially with the influx of immigrants, new ideas were welcomed including suffrage and the ladies were willing to work hard in campaigning to reap the fruits of their labor.

In 1890 the two organizations joined back together and now were known as NAWSA (National American Woman Suffrage Association) thinking it would bring unity and new states into the suffrage column, but the success did not appear. It did give the organization unity of work and a central organization but not new states.

Sadly, by 1900 there were only four western states that had suffrage-Wyoming-1869, Utah-1873, Colorado-1893, and Idaho-1896. State after state had voted against suffrage. There had been 480 state campaigns held from 1860 -1900 and 424 failed and the suffragists asked why?

These campaigns were expensive to develop and cumbersome with all the work involved. There were possibly 100,000 posters, 50,000 buttons, 18 banners, and 2,528,000 pieces of literature that were used in these campaigns. Petitions were sent to the legislatures of the states numbering hundreds of thousands of names. The cost of each campaign ran around $30,000 was supplied by national and state along the with physical presence of women to help. This was not the total for all the campaigns just a few. Do the math for 480 campaigns; add the cost and work and the total is almost unimaginable. Some women felt that the state by state campaigns were not working.

THE TACTICS OF THE BREWERS

Charging a Hat or Coat

It was exposed that immigrants, not yet citizens, had been allowed to vote or even paid to vote no for suffrage and temperance. Who was paying them? And there was the crux of the problem. After all the money that had been poured into these campaigns, the suffragists realized the insidious role of the Brewer's Association.

The Brewer's Association had made it very clear as early as 1860 that they had no reticence about using any means to eliminate both the Temperance and Suffrage groups as competition in their plans. It was collusion plain and simple. What they found was a systematic plan of what had occurred in all the suffrage campaigns where it was consistently voted down. The person who organized the anti-temperance and anti-suffrage was the same person in both cases. They kept their actions secret as much as it was possible from both groups which amounted to years. They destroyed most records of their dealings to carry out their plan. They set up accounts from which the money would be taken and handed out for payment. Saloons were given a quota of negative votes needed to defeat the referendums. Everything they did, by agreement of all, would be kept secret and hidden from the temperance and suffrage forces. Both movements received the same treatment.

Any man who was pro suffrage or temperance would be boycotted and particularly candidates for office. Lists were given in each election of good candidates those against temperance and suffrage. Either party was acceptable. In any election support would go to those candidates. They contacted every possible source to manipulate and follow their course of action.

In the legislatures, they chose the senate first because there were less men in that body of government. They picked committees where a referendum was first discussed. Approximately ¾ of the bills never reached the floor with such excuses as they were overworked, or the calendar was just too full to add it. One person can block what bills come out of committee thus suffrage bills were defeated right there. And the same thing can still happen today. If the speaker of the house does not want a bill to come out of committee, it can be held back and killed.

If the bill managed to get out of committee for a full vote, then came the other tactics. First were the subtle promises to help in the future, presents were sent to their wives or gifts to relatives or friends, and if that failed to bring the desired result, then came the bribery in dollars, coercion, intimidation, threats, or even physical confrontation.

The suffragists began to learn the signs and as they had always done, they wrote down what they saw and heard, and all these reports were sent to national. They kept fifty years of reports that basically told the same story. They learned that druggists, railroads, textiles, and manufacturers were also involved in this complex arrangement.

Each state had its own budget getting their own money and allocated it to individuals or groups as needed. No other state knew what they were doing, nor any one individual knew all the facts. They would charge fees for a barrel of liquor. One man from the Brewer's Association would be the agent in the state and it was usually the same man who would distribute to anti-prohibition and suffrage groups. If more assessments were needed, then an additional tax was added to make up the difference. In 1913 there was an additional tax of $.03 that was to run for five years which gave around $25 million of money for the Brewers to dole out to the states.

Of course, there were no records kept but it was estimated how much money there was by what was happening. In 1914 there were seven states that had referendums: five failed. Only Nevada and Montana succeeded in getting suffrage. If they assessed 3 cents per barrel, that would give them

$1.4 million. If there were fees of $100,000, it would still leave the rest for distribution; the money was channeled into the coffers and not directly given to campaigns. The money did not go into a central treasury where it could be tracked. This was enough for investigation. It was assumed that the dollar amount was ten times that amount but that was a guess. There was a concealment of their activities and they would record the congressmen who were and were not opposed to prohibition or suffrage.

What the Brewers also did was to take money and pay the fees of the immigrants to help them become naturalized citizens or they paid them to vote illegally and in the case of those who could not read, someone went with the man and showed him where to mark the ballot. From 1896-1911 no new states entered the union or voted for suffrage. This was done in California, Oregon, Arizona, Kansas, Montana, Nevada, North and South Dakota, Oklahoma, Texas, Missouri, Iowa, Nebraska, Wisconsin, and Michigan; these were states that had voted down suffrage and prohibition again and again although Montana and Nevada did win. By registering the Germans or other foreign non-citizens, anywhere from 70,000 to 300,000 votes were added to the polls in these states. This was the invincible political power or as it was appearing to the suffragists.

Women did not have the power to bring suits against the group. You can see what it did to the suffrage movement. Most felt that it added twenty years in getting suffrage. We have millions of illegals in this country now. Are they being allowed to vote in this country without being citizens to influence political control?

With what NAWSA had gathered in those fifty years of affidavits as evidence, the government began to indict and prosecute the offenders. The Attorney General of Texas sued seven breweries on January 9, 1915 for using their corporate assets in unlawful spending in politics and action that were contrary to the laws.

One hundred Pennsylvania breweries were indicted March 19, 1916 for unlawful spending of money in elections and influencing the voting outcome which was also illegal. They didn't fight the lawsuits; they settled and just agreed to pay the $1 million fine. The top officials were put on the stand and questioned in each case. Their defense in all questioning was lack of remembering what had occurred. They remembered nothing because the records had been destroyed; there were no minutes. Did this not also happen to emails recently in our government that had disappeared? There were no cancelled checks or records of their financial operations as those had also been destroyed. When questioned their constant comment was "I cannot recall" over and over thus avoiding the truth. What organization does not keep records of their activities unless they were trying to hide their exploits with the express purpose of hiding their complicity in fraudulent and criminal activities?

The Judiciary Committee of the U. S. Senate carried out an investigation in 1918. This is what they concluded, "The United States Brewers' Association, brewing companies, and allied interests have in recent years made contributions to political campaigns on a scale without precedent... and in order to control legislation in state and nation have exacted pledges from candidates in office... have subsidized the press and stipulated when contracting for advertising space with the newspapers that a certain amount be editorial space, the material to be furnished by the brewers' central office...they have set in operation an extensive system of boycotting...tabulating men and forces for and against them, and that they have paid large sums of money to citizens of the United States to advocate their cause, including some in government employ"[42]

---

[42] Suffrage and Politics, p.135

When the suffragists had questioned the senators during the campaigns, some would admit there may have been some unethical procedures but they usually revealed nothing because this political machine had so tied their hands and they needed a job and most feared the power they held over them particularly the propaganda and power of the German Alliance of the brewers and newspapers. The alliance was started in 1901, chartered in 1907 and it was taken away in 1918. There were over 700 German newspapers in the U.S. who used their papers to defeat suffrage in states again and again and bragged about how they did it in all states.

These criminal procedures did not alleviate the actions of the Brewer's Association. This was an early political machine that used the power of money and politics to control actions; it will continue even while the states are in the process of ratifying the 19th amendment, even to the very last day.

Now Carrie Chapman Catt as a high official knew about this episode of history; she even wrote a book about it called Politics and Suffrage, the story behind the mission. She waited till after the amendment had passed revealing all the events the workers had kept as evidence even the letters that were handed to the suffragists in Montana proving that the anti-suffragists and the Brewer's Association were working in league with each other.

Carrie Chapman Catt

In 1914 a letter given to the suffragists and marked confidential said this," In regard to the matter of woman suffrage, we are trying to keep from having any connection with it whatever. We are, however, in a position to establish channels of communication with the leaders of the anti-suffrage movement for our friend in any state where suffrage is an issue. . . .I consider it most dangerous to have the (liquor) retailers identified or active in and in this fight, as it will be used against us everywhere."[43]

---

[43] Woman's Suffrage Movement, p.86

This was the proof that the anti-suffrage forces were working with the liquor interests. The anti-forces had organized in 1882 and in 1900 eight states had anti suffrage organizations and there were twenty by 1920. The official name was the NAOWS-National Association Opposed to Women Suffrage. Mostly upper middle- class women were the head of these groups. Their biggest and most used arguments included that women were being forced by the suffragists and did not want to vote. They voiced the idea that it would destroy the family and that voting was not the natural state of women or the women's sphere as it was also called. The anti-suffragists would also be there until the final vote. It did not stop the suffragists!

Charging a Hat or Coat

TWO VIEWPOINTS OF SUFFFRAGE - CATT AND PAUL

Charging a Hat or Coat

The impetus to move forward with a national amendment continued in both organizations-NAWSA and NWP. Alice Paul believed in a small central leadership with a chairman and two committee members. They felt this was better as you had less people to get to acquiesce on policy eliminating some of the many minds. There was no voting and thus easier to implement.

The CU blamed the Democrats and Woodrow Wilson for not passing the suffrage amendment. Wilson believed it should be up to the states to pass the amendment. Alice Paul blamed the Democratic Party for this policy and set out to campaign against them in the next election in 1914 and they concentrated on the western states of Washington, Idaho, California, Arizona, Kansas, Wyoming, Nevada, Utah, Colorado, and Oregon.

Aaron Sargent first introduced the suffrage amendment in 1876 to Congress and it was rejected periodically throughout the years. It was once again introduced in 1914 and rejected. The southern democrats were a big force behind the failure.

The next step Alice Paul took was the emphasis of making suffrage a national issue. By the end of 1915, there were CU chapters in nineteen states.   Again South Dakota, Iowa and West Virginia lost the suffrage vote.

Carrie Chapman Catt had returned as president of NAWSA. She took over an organization that was sharply divided due to the former president Anna Howard Shaw; there was also dissension and disagreement between Carrie Chapman Catt and Alice Paul. The younger suffragists challenged the strategies and tactics of the older women.

Alice Paul intended to have a national convention at the Panama Pacific Exposition to be held in San Francisco. Hazel Hunkins Hallinan who was a Vassar graduate flew in a plane and dropped leaflets over the convention. The Ford Assembly line produced an 18-foot petition that people were going to sign so that it could be sent to Washington, D. C. and presented to Congress and to the President, Woodrow Wilson. It did not bring the result that was expected so it was dropped.

Alice Paul gave up her anti-democratic campaign and planned no future campaigns; her only mission at this point was obtaining suffrage. In 1916, there were only twelve suffrage states. The NWP established a national office in Washington, D.C. known as the Little White House. It was in the Cameron House just across the street from the White House on Pennsylvania Avenue. This was the hub of the CU. Only members of the CU were members of the NWP. It was to be an independent organization with no attachment to any political party.

Anne Martin of Nevada and Maude Younger, a millionaire from California, were using their expertise and influence to get the suffrage amendment out of the Judiciary Committee. They were the liaisons from the NWP and key lobbyists Alice Paul had working in Congress. They were very good in what they did; Maud Younger had proved this by single handedly starting a waitress union in San Francisco, California. The union got an eight-hour workday for waitresses.

To further expand efforts on the suffrage bill, around twenty-three women from the NWP party lived and worked on the train called the "Suffrage Special". They went out west urging people to support suffrage and get involved.

Teddy Roosevelt, who was running for the Progressive Party, did support the federal amendment. Teddy Roosevelt had been a president but was not selected by the Democratic Party, so he turned to the Progressive Party which he had formed. Alice Paul and Carrie Chapman Catt wanted his support and the Republican nominee. Charles Evans Hughes also supported suffrage, but it did not make the platform of the party. The NWP worked against the Democrats. The party used the slogan "He kept us out of the war". The NWP used their slogan "He kept us out of suffrage"

Woodrow Wilson

The NAWSA convention had Woodrow Wilson as the featured speaker. Carrie Chapman Catt considered Woodrow Wilson as a friendly associate and worked well with him; she was a good organizer and politician. They had developed a new "winning plan". This plan included getting a national suffrage law on both the state and national level and partial suffrage in states resisting change and primary suffrage in the southern states. By this process NAWSA won the support of both the U.S. House and Senate.

Woodrow Wilson supported the Adamson eight-hour day, Keating-Owens Labor Law, Rural credits and Federal Workman's Compensation Law which he had not supported in 1912. Wilson won the election by a close call of 277-254 which the Democrats felt was because of the suffragists. The election recognized the power of women and the democratic leaders realized they need to incorporate these ideas before the next election.

But there was still dissension between the NAWSA group and the NWP. The new group was more militant and impatient; the new term for them was suffragettes. They included Harriet Stanton Blatch (Elizabeth Stanton's daughter), Alva Vanderbilt Belmont, Phoebe Hearst, and others. NAWSA members felt that the CU was trying to take over; the two organizations were still clashing over dominance. Now we can look back at the situation and see what maybe should have been done but wasn't. Carrie Chapman Catt had been working for suffrage all her life and said she felt that the struggle would be her life's work which it was with her working even after the 19th amendment passed as law.

Alice Paul was young as were others in the NWP and tired of waiting and dissatisfied with the present goals. She also considered suffrage as part of her life's work and like Catt worked to the end of her life. They had witnessed the policy of militant action in England by Emmeline Pankhurst and felt it was achieving faster results. Emmeline Pankhurst was the same age as Carrie Chapman Catt but with differing views. Both Alice Paul and Carrie Chapman Catt were very strong-willed women; this ultimately brought disagreement between them.

If you recall Alice Paul returned to the United States in 1910. By this time four pioneers of the suffrage movement had died: Lucretia Mott (1880), Lucy Stone Blackwell (1893}, Elizabeth Cady Stanton, (1902), and Susan Brownell Anthony (1906). These women had worked together through the years and they were closer in age and experience except Lucretia Mott who was twenty years older.

Between Carrie Chapman Catt and Alice Paul, there was a notable age difference. Probably Catt and some of the others felt she was an upstart whereas they had been working and trying different methods and spent numerous hours writing letters, seeking petitions, campaigns, talking to committees, giving speeches, and traveling to suffrage meetings all over the country and they became outstanding organizers! The suffragettes had barely started but were critical of their elders. Both sides continued the fight which now included only getting a national suffrage amendment and Alice Paul was very adamant on this point. This was the disagreement and what methods were used to obtain this result.

On June 7, 1916 over 5,000 suffragettes from the NWP marched in pouring rain to the Republican National Convention in Chicago, Illinois to present a plea to include suffrage in their platform. The anti-suffragists were beginning their speech saying that women did not want the vote when the 5,000 drenched women, members of the NWP marched into the meeting room. The speaker was so flustered that she could not continue. Men had lined up eight and ten deep watching them walk to the convention hall. One man standing there noted the determination of the women marching and felt they might as well support them. It was also the city where NWP was holding their convention which made it convenient.

On June 14, 1916, in St. Louis, Missouri, another demonstration at the Democratic Convention repeated what had happened in Chicago by the NWP. Here the ladies were dressed all in white with gold sashes and holding yellow parasols with signs of Votes for Women. They were in a long line on Locust Street. There was no violence; the ladies quietly stood to prompt the convention members to endorse suffrage in their platform.

Charging a Hat or Coat

WORLD WAR I AND SUFFRAGE

Charging a Hat or Coat

In 1917, the U.S. entered W.W. I and after much thought Carrie Chapman Catt abandoned her peace effort and supported the war. She had started the Women's Peace Party in 1915 but Woodrow Wilson had asked her to head an organization to feed and help the soldiers on the front. There were food shortages, so people were asked to plant gardens to feed the people. They set up butter-less and wheat-less days. As the men went to fight in the war, workers were needed in the factories. Women stepped in to fill the jobs and daycare was needed to take care of the children while the mothers worked. Members of NAWSA volunteered to help along with other jobs of providing clothes, hats and gloves for the soldiers fighting overseas. The public was impressed with these efforts and looked on suffrage groups with a much more favorable view even considering them patriotic. Woodrow Wilson even asked Congress to consider the federal suffrage amendment; the Congress refused to put it on the agenda.

And with that dismissal by Congress, on the morning of January 10, 1917, three hundred suffragettes formed a single line near the White House to picket. They were called the "silent sentinels." Mabel Vernon was the key organizer of the group. They formed a line and stood around the White House six days a week. This was the new technique Alice Paul used to get suffrage in the news. Harriet Stanton Blatch also used this technique in New York and was successful in getting suffrage for that state. They would become the first group in American History to use this form of protest.

Mabel Vernon coordinated the picket calling for women to volunteer for shifts of duty and the response was very gratifying. Over 2,000 women took turns on the line. They could picket an hour or however much they arranged. There were a few like Josephine DuPont who considered it undignified but still sent a $l,000 check. There were certain days for states-Maryland Day, Pennsylvania, New York Day. Woodrow Wilson would have his head usher go out and inquire on cold days to offer tea or coffee to the ladies, but they absolutely refused any offers. The purpose of the picket was to get the papers to get coverage for their actions and there were certainly write-ups in the papers even though Wilson would later ask them to suppress coverage to the back pages. Woodrow Wilson would tip his hat to the ladies as he came through the gate.

In early February, the Germans carried out unrestricted warfare which meant they attacked all ships on the water whether military or trading ships. Alice Paul called for a state convention to discuss their position if war were declared. Woodrow Wilson then severed all diplomatic relations with Germany. The day before Wilson was to be inaugurated, the picket line around the White House found that the gate was locked, and the guards refused to take any resolutions. The weather that day was icy rain. War was declared on April 6 and Congress would only conduct war measures nothing else and suffrage was not considered a war measure.

Alice Paul

NAWSA supported the call for war. Jeanette Rankin, first woman congresswomen, was a pacifist even though members of NAWSA pressured her to vote for war which she failed to do. She was not reelected. She lost her seat in Congress and was not elected to Congress again until 1940 where she again refused to vote for W.W. II. NAWSA turned against her, but Alice Paul supported her position. Alice Paul did not consider the war an important issue to stop working for suffrage. The suffragists had done this during the Civil War and lost support.

In June 1917 the Espionage Act passed Congress as a means of punishing those who were believed to be committing acts of treason by picketing. Judge Muldowney wanted to use this act on the picketing women to put them in jail. It was also an issue that middleclass women were being arrested and thrown in jail. It did not look appropriate that the U.S. was fighting for democracy in Europe but throwing American women in jail.

With the passage of the Espionage Act, Major Raymond Pullman called Alice Paul and warned her of possible arrests if the pickets were not stopped. Alice then called the ladies who would picket and warned them of this possible result and left it to them to decide if they would continue or not. Alice Paul thought they would be protected by the Clayton Act which it apparently did not as another call reached Paul about the arrest of Lucy Burns and Katherine Morey. The two ladies were not arrested but fined.

The police arrested 27 more women in the time from June 22-26 and charged them with obstruction of traffic; they were released without penalty. The police thought the arrests would halt the pickets, but no such thing occurred. On June 27, six more picketers were arrested and put on trial and fined $25 which they refused to pay and were given three-day jail sentences. They had decent cells with running water and restrooms. More arrests occurred resulting in the same action.

The public was becoming increasing intolerant of the pickets now that war had been declared. They tore down the banners that the women held on the picket line and the police did nothing. The banners were considered seditious material and treasonous during the war. The picketers burned the speeches Woodrow Wilson had given in urns saying he was working for democracy in Europe and denying it to women in the United States.

Arthur Brisbane of the **Washington Times** spoke to the NWP about the picketing. He promised daily front news coverage if they stopped the picketing. They rejected his offer. Charles A. Lindbergh wrote the president saying the ladies had a constitutional right to picket; it did not stop the pickets nor the arrests.

The next group of sixteen women, arrested on July 14 were not as privileged. These women on July 14 were tried and sentenced to Occoquan, Virginia for sixty days in a workhouse for failure to pay a $25 fine. They were sentenced before Judge Muldowney who had wanted harsher sentences by the Espionage Act that had passed Congress. The women he sentenced were Doris Stevens, Anne Martin, Florence Bayard Hills, and Mrs. John Rogers. Florence Hills said "I stand here to affirm my innocence of the charge against me. . . This court has not proven that I obstructed traffic. During the months of January, February, March, April, and May picketing was legal. In June it suddenly becomes illegal."[44]

Anne Martin, who was her own consul, said "As long as the government and the representatives of the government prefer to send women to jail on petty and technical charges, we will go to jail. Persecution has always advanced the cause of justice. . . our work for the passage of the amendment must go on. It will go on."[45]

---

[44] Jailed for Freedom, p. 324
[45] Jailed for Freedom, 324

Dudley Field Malone had worked for Woodrow Wilson in helping him get elected in both elections of 1912 and 1916. In the latter election of 1916, he had gone west to get women to vote for Wilson in states that had suffrage, particularly California. He talked to the ladies and promised to work for the suffrage amendment even though Wilson had not helped get the amendment through Congress. It was this state that had helped get victory for Wilson as it was a close election. "To me, Mr. President as I urged upon you in Washington two months ago, this is not only a measure of justice and democracy, it is also an urgent war measure."[46] Malone tried to mediate between the opposing sides urging Woodrow Wilson to accept the suffrage amendment into law.

On July 20 Woodrow Wilson did pardon the arrested suffragettes and allowed them to keep picketing. Charles Evans Hughes had given his support for the Susan B. Anthony suffrage amendment and now so did Woodrow Wilson. To help the soldiers in the war, Camp Americanism was started for war activities getting or making socks, gloves, and mufflers for the boys at the front. Care baskets were also made and shipped to the soldiers and at home, victory gardens sprang up to feed them. Women took over jobs usually done by

[46] Jailed for Freedom, 325

men who were now fighting in Europe. Here is where women took over being secretaries since the men were gone.

The pickets and arrests continued all day; there was physical abuse on the picket line and the police did nothing.   The suffragettes were given longer sentences and psychological warfare was used for inducing terror in the women; this was the decree of the superintendent of prisons, Raymond Whitacre. So now the prisoners were placed among the regular prisoners including the men. The sanitation and air in the prison was putrid and foul smelling. One woman killed three rats in her cell beating them off her cot.   The food was barely edible and scarce. The ladies had a contest to see who had the most mealworms in their food.

The second part of the psychological process was that they allowed them no contact with the outside world with no mail and no visitors.   If mail was sent to them, it was returned to the sender; they were not allowed due process of law.   Yet the suffragettes were still picketing outside the White House. In October and November, the harshest sentences yet were imposed; Alice Paul was given seven months after being arrested for picketing and Rose Winslow-six months at Occoquan. Their lawyer, Lucy Burns attempted to get them classified as political prisoners and that was rejected. They tried to smuggle information to the district authorities. Their whereabouts were unknown so they could not confer with either of them. Each began a hunger strike in protest.

Both ladies were force fed for three weeks three times a day. What that meant was that each was tied or held down by five people in a chair and food was given them to them through tubes put in their nostrils or through their throats and running to their stomachs. Mostly the women threw up from this treatment, but it was not stopped. No visitors were allowed including Alice's lawyer, Dudley Field Moore, nor were they allowed to receive mail. Alice even had her windows boarded up with no light being allowed. Her comment about this, "At night, in the early morning, all through the day, there were cries and shrieks and moans from the patients. It was terrifying. One particularly horrifying moan hour after hour used to keep me up with the regularity of a heartbeat. I said to myself, 'Now I have to endure this. I have got to live through this somehow. I'll pretend these moans are the noise of an elevated train, beginning faintly in the distance and getting louder as it comes nearer' Such childish devices were useful to me."[47]

---

[47] From Equal Suffrage to Equal Rights, p. 133

Alice Paul incurred special treatment in that she was in the psychopathic ward; she was allowed absolutely no visitors or mail. The door was taken off her room and every hour on the hour, she was awakened by having a bright light flashed in her face. She had to be interviewed by a psychiatrist questioning her again and again about her personal feelings for Woodrow Wilson to get her to admit she hated him and had a persecution mania. She was put in a strait jacket. Thus, they could call her delusional and homicidal. The purpose of this intense interrogation was to impugn the sanity of Alice Paul. Remember when Susan Anthony was put on trial, it was to break her spirit by the treatment. The nurses who attended to Paul assured her that she was not insane.

Some of this treatment was reaching the outside and complaints were made to Woodrow Wilson. Alice Paul had this to say "I believe I have never in my life before feared anything or any human-being. But I confess I was afraid of Dr. Gannon, the jail physician. I dreaded the hour of his visit; he said 'I will show you who rules this place. You think you do. But I will show you are wrong."[48]

---

[48] From Equal Suffrage to Equal Rights, p. 133

Woodrow Wilson upon hearing the complaints about the treatment of the prisoners sent a representative, David Lawrence, to attest to the events. He interviewed Alice Paul and asked her if she would abandon the picketing if she and the other persons were released. Her answer was only the passage of the federal suffrage amendment would be adequate. The pickets continued.

Then came the cataclysmic night on November 14, 1917. It was given the title "Night of Terrors" Five hundred women were arrested and one hundred and sixty-eight were jailed and brought into the holding room. Richard Whitacre, the superintendent of the prison and fifteen to forty guards rushed into the room and began manhandling the women. Mary Nolan, a 73-year-old woman with a bad leg was grabbed by two guards and dragged to a cell. Dorothy Day had her arm twisted behind her back; Dora Lewis was thrown in the jail cell and was knocked unconscious. Alice Cosu was also thrown in the cell and had a heart attack as a result. Lucy Burns had manacles binding her hands and was handcuffed to the top of the cell by her arms. To humiliate her even more they removed all her clothes. She was the suffragette who earned the notoriety of having spent the most days in jail through picketing. After all this was over and the amendment passed, this was what she said "I don't want to do anything more. I think we have done all this for women, and we have sacrificed everything we possessed for them and now let them fight for it now. I am not going to fight anymore."[49] Brutality was the order of business for this group of prisoners! Woodrow Wilson got the news of what had happened but refused to admit that the women were being treated so maliciously.

Lucy Burns

NWP engineered a "Prison Special" train to cross the country to inform people of the treatment

---

[49] From Equal Suffrage to Equal Rights, p. 152, Lunardi Quotes Wikipedia

that the women had endured or were enduring while in jail. Former prisoners wore garments as they had in jail or showed the results of their treatment. Others had also suffered this treatment and smuggled out scraps of papers telling the truth of their ordeal. There were numerous affidavits of prisoners and what they had been subjected to in prison, including being kicked and beaten. This was what was told on the train trip. Outcries from the public, congressional leaders, and newspapers brought the truth and finally, all prisoners were released on November 30, 1918.

Bradley Malone found where Alice Paul was being kept isolated. He used a writ of habeas corpus to get her released from psychiatric evaluations and treatment where she was also allowed regular visitors. After this most sentences were only eight days. From November 29 to January,1919 there was still picketing from time to time. There were also a series of appeals going through the courts and the government was being charged with denying 1st amendment rights to all the women who had been arrested. The Bill of Rights protects us, but people can and do abuse those rights to force people to bend to their demands. Another sad fact about this incident was that NASWA was quiet about what was happening.

Another meeting in Layette Park saw forty-eight women arrested with several sentences being up to fifteen days in a facility that had previously been closed but was opened again for these prisoners. There was a hunger strike and protest till their release was gained; there was still picketing, and the speeches of Woodrow Wilson were burned in urns as a protest.

Another suffrage vote was to be rescheduled by Senator Jones for late September and he promised it would stay active until it passed. A House Suffrage committee had been opened and would stay open. At this time Woodrow Wilson asked to speak before the Senate which had rarely happened. In his speech, he encouraged the Senate to vote for suffrage as it was necessary to prove to the world that the people of the U.S. were not hypocrites in fighting for democracy in Europe but denying American women the right to vote. It was now considered a war measure to be passed by Congress, but it was rejected.

THE 19TH AMENDMENT PASSES! NEXT-RATIFICATION

Charging a Hat or Coat

The pressure did not cease, and the public became involved also. Even NAWSA was cooperating. Woodrow Wilson called in 12 congressmen to encourage an affirmative vote on suffrage. Finally, the House passed the 19th Amendment on May 21, 1919 with a vote of 304 - 89. The Senate followed on June 4, 1919; the 19th amendment became a law of Congress. That was the first step; now the second step was getting thirty-six states to ratify it. It would take fifteen months.

Carrie Chapman Catt, upon learning of the victory, immediately sent telegrams to all the governors of the full suffrage states asking for special sessions and if the legislatures were in session to immediately ratify the amendment. In nineteen days, nine states had ratified the amendment. Both NAWSA and NWP were excellent organizers and NAWSA had in place the schedule of getting ratification. Both groups were in juxtaposition ready to get the amendment passed in thirty-six states. They had used petitions before ratification and when the amendment passed, the states were to proceed with getting ratification

The suffrage movement is a prime example of democracy in action. It had been a fight taking seventy-two years involving two million or more women some more proactive than others. Even the small efforts helped the cause like the woman who said she would walk to work and donate her car fare. The small amounts of money given grew into large amounts along with wealthy women who donated large amounts. This was a grassroots operation. Now the all-male congresses in the state legislatures who were needed to achieve this goal had to be persuaded to vote for suffrage.

The struggle, not yet over, but was much closer in sight. Some women knew nothing about suffrage and more women worked tirelessly against it. Ten states did not ratify one of them being Delaware in the north and the other nine southern states-Virginia being one of those. Think of that! Virginia the scene of so much fervor and action in the pre-revolutionary events with leaders such as Patrick Henry and Thomas Jefferson, rejects the right of women getting suffrage. Major leaders of the revolution and four of the first five presidents of the United States came from this state. Those presidents were George Washington, Thomas Jefferson, James Madison, and James Monroe. Yet they rejected the freedom of vote to one half of the population. You would think that a state with that much influence would hold true to the Constitution.

The amendment needed thirty-six states to make it a law. Ratification was still a problem. The opposition needed thirteen states to stop the amendment and that was their goal. The two organizations were still arguing between themselves; there were still the militants, and of course the anti-suffragists. The state legislatures had other agendas besides ratification and rest assured the Brewer's Association was ready and waiting with money and tactics to implement any action against the states attempting to ratify the 19th amendment. NAWSA had the best organization in all the states; they had built the framework over many years of campaigns.

Forty-eight state legislatures met in the fall of 1919. Twenty-two of them were expected to ratify the amendment though all considered the Southern ratification hopeless though they did try hard. Carrie Chapman Catt held conferences and training sessions to help the attempt. The western states were slow to ratify since most of them already had suffrage for women. Catt appealed to them to ratify the 19th amendment even though the women in their states could already vote. Telegrams and wires were sent to those states that were dragging their feet in calling their legislatures. Montana was the first western state to ratify the 19th amendment; it was the first state to elect a woman to congress, Jeanette Rankin. She voted against W.W.I. Illinois, Michigan, and Wisconsin were the first three states to ratify the 19th amendment because they were still in session and could easily organize the material and vote on ratification.

Four states in the north that failed to ratify before the deadline were Delaware, Connecticut, Vermont, and West Virginia. Telegrams were sent to all four governors to call emergency special sessions. All four governors replied that they could see no reason for calling one. All were opposed to the 19th amendment even though most women were in favor of it.

An example of one of these states was Connecticut. The campaign for ratification was called the emergency corps and cost $5,000. Forty-eight women composed of doctors, lawyers, scientists, professors held a meeting May 2,1920. They were divided into four groups of twelve each and went out to the chief cities to give speeches. They then divided into more groups and went to small cities to do the same. They were in thirty-six towns and held forty-one meetings. On May 7 at 11:30 they were in the capitol giving speeches to the governor; his reaction was that he had to think about it. His answer in four days was he did not consider this an emergency. The women then proceeded to boycott the Republican Party by refusing to work for the party. This was the same process for the other three states with the same result as Connecticut with no ratification until after the 19th amendment had already been declared law.

No states along the eastern seaboard which had been part of the confederacy ratified the 19th amendment. Every state that was anti-suffrage used the excuse that it interfered with their states' rights. The southern states that rejected the amendment were Alabama, Georgia, Virginia, North and South Carolina, Mississippi, Maryland, Louisiana, and Florida.

The governor of Louisiana started an organization of thirteen to reject the 19th Amendment but then they decided to have rejection resolutions. The rejection resolution read basically the same for each state "Resolved by the General Assembly of the State of . . . .the House and Senate concurring that the proposed amendment to the Constitution of the United States be, and hereby is, rejected as an unwarranted, unnecessary, undemocratic and dangerous interference with the rights reserved to the States or to the people in both State and Federal Constitution, and be it further, ... Resolved, that we call upon our sister States of the

Union to uphold and defend the right of each State to decide who shall vote for its own officers, and to oppose and reject any amendment to the Constitution of the United States that would transfer control of State franchises to the Federal Congress without the consent of the people themselves as duly exercised under their several State Constitutions."[50]

Georgia and Alabama were the first states to defeat the amendment. In Alabama and Virginia, the liquor forces were openly working against ratification.   South Carolina had the suffrage amendment rejected in the Senate and withdrawn from the House as it would be defeated there too. They did not want the vote for women by any means. The Virginia legislature had sixty-one new members and had passed the Prohibition amendment so were against any new federal amendment. On February 6, the rejection resolution passed in the Senate and on the 12th in the House. On March 12, a qualifications resolution was introduced into the legislature letting the women vote by the federal amendment already passed by the U.S. Congress. It took two legislative sessions in order to get it passed which meant the

---

[50] Suffrage and Politics, p. 463

national amendment gave them the vote. The democratic legislators ignored all telegrams, letters, and petitions from suffrage supporters in defiance.

Maryland refused to even call a special legislative session then set dates for one but changed the date; people were unable to appear and speak for passage. Even in the new government, a rejection resolution was passed. The legislative assembly in Florida was still in session and had passed the 18th amendment but failed to ratify the suffrage amendment. They took no action. It was a fact that every state that failed to ratify the suffrage amendment did ratify the 18th (Prohibition) amendment. Louisiana was expected to pass the amendment, but the suffragists delegates turned against the vote due to the policy of states' rights and followed the will of the state. There was still much bitterness in the south from the Civil War.

Because the 19th amendment was ratified by thirty-six states, all women who were registered to vote went to the polls in the November election of 1920 except Georgia and Mississippi. Their state laws required that people be registered six months in Georgia and four months in Mississippi which was too late for the election.

Eventually all the above states did ratify the 19th amendment. Maryland passed it in 1941, Virginia in 1952, Alabama in 1953, Florida and South Carolina in 1969, Georgia and Louisiana in 1970, North Carolina in 1971, and Mississippi in 1984. The women had voted all this time; apparently the legislatures rejected it as a statement, but the women still had the right.

Now Tennessee was a unique state and intense lobbying procured the votes by NAWSA and NWP for suffrage. Carrie Chapman Catt was the head of the NAWSA delegation and Sue Shelton White was the NWP representative. Shelton was a Tennessee native and member of the "Prison Special" train that had traveled over the country explaining the altercation between the women and police over the picketing and arrests and their treatment. Even though these organizations had dissension with each other, they still had the same goal of getting ratification and worked together.

The governor of Tennessee was in favor of ratification. Many of the legislators were undecided about which side they would take so all interested parties met the trains in which they arrived. Their action became known as the "War of Roses". Yellow roses were given out for the representatives in favor of suffrage and red for the anti-suffrage. Delegates were besieged with ladies defending one side or the other from morning to night. The Brewers Association was still very busy taking groups of men into meetings. On the morning of the voting the ladies noticed that some men were clearly intoxicated or hungover. The suffrage ladies knew exactly what had happened since the liquor forces and the anti-suffragists were still in league with each other. The men had been offered old bourbon and moonshine whiskey, free liquor in exchange for a negative vote.

Finally, on August 12, 1920 the Senate voted 24-5 in favor of the amendment. The critical House vote was held August 18 even though some men tried to table it. Harry Burn held the critical vote and had been threatened over an alleged bribe if he voted in favor of suffrage. Five minutes before the vote was to be taken, Harry Burn received a note which was from his mother asking him to vote for ratification. He did as she asked, and the rest is history. The final tally was sent by registered mail to Washington, D.C. to the Secretary of State. Officially the amendment was ratified on August 18, 1920 and the document was sent to the Congress where it was certified and recorded.

The United States became the twenty-seventh country to vote for women suffrage. Twenty-six million women were now enfranchised by this action and the voting bloc feared by many men never appeared to affect elections.

The southern states also filed lawsuits against the thirty-six states who had ratified. Their reasoning was that the vote was invalid and needed to be set aside. The cases went to the Supreme Court and were rejected. One senator said, "we opponents of the Amendment are trying to save the women of Georgia from the repetition of reconstruction days. It is not a question of woman suffrage but a question of protecting Georgia womanhood. ... Women should not be allowed to vote. Their privilege and obligation is to bear children. ...Women are now refusing to bear children because of the policy of woman suffrage. ... women who vote came here to induce Georgia women to refuse to bear children which was the sole aim and end for having women at all according to the Bible doctrine.[51] Are you laughing yet? If the only purpose of women was to bear children, then that means they should not have helped farm, make butter, spin cotton, make clothes, sew, wash, cook, or anything else. By federal law all the women in these states could vote.

---

[51] Suffrage and Politics, p. 467

Before the Secretary of State signed the 19th Amendment into law, there was a meeting on March 19, 1919 in St. Louis, Missouri and in 1920 held jointly with the last national women's convention, the formation of a new group by Carrie Chapman Catt called the League of Woman Voters. It was to help women be informed with what was going on in politics. It was meant to keep them active and working for the rights of women; it was supposed to be non-partisan but with political parties, that is hard to sustain.

Women were promised great things with the right to vote but no riches were at the end of the rainbow. The older suffragists thought the younger ones should take up the mantra and work for the other things but the "flapper girl" came into focus in the 20's. Remember the Prohibition Amendment(18th) had also passed and alcohol was abolished or supposed to be but instead it continued to be made illegally. The jobs were not suddenly better and open to all women; there were still many discrepancies among men and women. One older woman suffragist (Gertrude Foster Brown) complained about the lack of women who didn't work hard as they had to get more equal rights for women. Her husband said "You did all this, you know. You wanted independence; you wanted rights; now you got them, and you can't complain if women don't choose to use them as you thought they would." Seneca Falls[52]

Here are the exact dates of ratification for those thirty-six states.

Illinois-June 10, 1919
Wisconsin-June 10, 1919
Michigan-June 10, 1919
Kansas-June 16, 1919
New York-June16, 1919
Ohio-June 16, 1919
Pennsylvania-June 24, 1919
Massachusetts-June 25, 1919
Texas-June 28, 1919
Iowa-July 2, 1919
Missouri-July 3, 1919
Arkansas-July 28, 1919
Montana-July 30, 1919
Nebraska-August 2, 1919
Minnesota-September 8, 1919
New Hampshire-September 10, 1919
Utah-September 30, 1919
California-November 1, 1919
Maine-November 5, 1919
North Dakota-December 1, 1919

---

[52] Wikipedia Life of Gertrude Foster Brown and Life of Husband of a Suffragette

South Dakota-December 4, 1919

Colorado-December 12, 1919

Kentucky-January 6, 1920

Rhode Island-January 6, 1920

Oregon-January 12, 1920

Indiana-January 16, 1920

Wyoming-January 26, 1920

Nevada-February 7, 1920

New Jersey-February 9, 1920

Idaho-February 11, 1920

Arizona-February 12, 1920

New Mexico-February 16, 1920

Oklahoma-February 23, 1920

West Virginia-March 10, 1920

Washington-March 22, 1920

Tennessee-August 18,1920

On February 12-18, 1920, the last suffrage convention was held in Chicago, Illinois; there had been fifty-one of these conventions. It was a terrible winter with lots of ice and snow and still the delegates came from Maine, Florida, California, Texas, and all over to celebrate this victory even though the amendment had not officially been passed by 36 states. There was a sense of jubilation to be there; a bell hung in the middle of the room with a satin ribbon and the women would ring the bell as they marched around the room when another state had ratified the 19th Amendment.

Announcements were made and called out as New Jersey, Indiana, Arizona, and New Mexico ratified the 19th amendment bringing the number of states ratifying to thirty-two. Telegrams were sent out in congratulations and notices went to the newspapers. Telegrams were also sent to Connecticut, Vermont, Delaware, and West Virginia urging them to call special sessions of their legislatures to ratify the amendment.

A big Valentine heart stood on a balcony in a frame. The states that had already ratified stood in the frame individually and told the story of their state and its ratification process.

There were commemorations for Anna Howard Shaw and Susan Anthony with pictures and their struggles working for suffrage. The delegates stayed on task developing plans for emergencies and setbacks in the remaining states.

When Susan retired from being president of NAWSA and eighty years old, a party was held in her honor and in part of her farewell address she referred to herself as "Once I was the most despised and hated woman in the world; now, it seems as if everybody loves me!"[53]

Even the southern delegates ratifying the 19th amendment referred to her as the worst enemy the South ever had. At this point she had been gone 14 years. Forgiveness was not on their agenda.

The party held for her was at the Corcoran Gallery of Art. She also received 3,000 letters from well -wishers and Elizabeth Cady Stanton's daughter read a letter from her mother recalling her history and wishing her well. Susan was well loved by the suffragists even in the rest of the world. Many referred to her as "Aunt Susan". Susan openly said how proud she was of the newer members and suffrage was in good hands.

A delegate from Wyoming brought her a brooch of a gold American flag with four diamonds referring to the states that had suffrage-Wyoming, Utah, Idaho, and Colorado. They then told her "We hope you may live to see all the common stars turn into diamonds."[54]

Susan went home to the family farm in Rochester, New York which her sister Mary had

---

[53] Ladies of Seneca Falls, p. 294

[54] Ladies of Seneca Falls, p. 293-4, History of Woman Suffrage, v. 4.

inherited. They renovated and redecorated the thirteen- room home from gifts that she had received over the years including the table from Seneca Falls. Mary did most of the work and it became Susan Anthony's headquarters as she kept working for suffrage. It was not uncommon for Susan to receive a thousand pieces of mail from both men and women asking for her opinions on everything. She rose at 6:00 A.M. and stayed up till 10:00 P.M. answering all the mail that she received.

Susan Anthony traveled to Berlin for the meeting of the International Council of Women and was enthusiastically greeted by the women who admired her there. Here at home in 1905 she went to Oregon to help implement support for Oregon's suffrage campaign which still failed. It was hard to beat the liquor industry who jubilantly bragged about their achievements.

In the last period of her life in 1906, she attended the national convention, her last convention in February even though she was ill. It was not expected that she would speak but she made the effort being the "grand old lady". As she was introduced, the audience rose and gave her a standing ovation for over ten minutes. This was her last speech at a convention. "This is a magnificent sight before me, and these have been wonderful addresses and speeches I have listened to during the past week. Yet I have looked on many such audiences and in my lifetime. I have listened to many such speakers all testifying to the righteousness, the justice and the worthiness of the cause of woman suffrage. I never saw that great woman Mary Wollstonecraft, but I have read her eloquent and unanswerable arguments on behalf of the liberty of womankind. I have met and known most of the progressive women who came after her- Lucretia Mott, the Grimke' sisters, Elizabeth Cady Stanton, Lucy Stone-a long galaxy of great women. I have heard them speak saying in only slightly different phrases what I heard these newer advocates of the cause say at these meetings. Those older women have gone on and most of those who worked with me in the early years have gone, I am here for a little time only and then my place will be filled as theirs was filled. The fight must not cease; you must see that it does not stop. Failure is not an option"[55] Susan passed away in March. Susan Anthony was the only suffragist to be honored by having a coin made in her honor.

The delegates returned home after the convention to get back to working to get the states not yet ratified in the yes column. Only four states

---

[55] History of Woman Suffrage, v. 56, p, 185

were needed to finish the job and it looked as if it were going to be a long journey. They had come this far and weren't going to admit defeat; they were confident they could reach their goal.

RATIFICATION AND THE AFTERMATH

Charging a Hat or Coat

The League of Women Voters which had been created developed a plan of operation. They wanted to help women learn how to choose good candidates and participate in the political process. They wanted to help get citizenship for new citizens and they wanted legislation for the protection for the women, children, and homes. This would be the continuance of the work started by the suffrage organizations. Maud Wood Park became the head of the organization in 1923.

This organization started by Carrie Chapman Catt was just one of the activities Catt was involved with after the passage of the 19th Amendment. In 1920, she also started the International Woman's Suffrage Alliance now called International Alliance of Women. From 1904-1923 she was the president and honorary president till her death. She and her friend, Jane Adams, founded the Woman's Peace Party. Catt had already started one in the early 1900's but had retreated from it in order to support Woodrow Wilson and World War I.

Not only did Carrie Chapman Catt establish the Peace Party but a "Committee for the Causes and Cures of War"; she was their chairwoman and was till 1932 and then the honorary chair for the rest of her life. She worked for Jewish refugees and urged Congress to allow the Jewish refugees to escape the horrors that were being implemented against the Jews in Europe. She was given the Jewish Medal of Honor for her help.

Carrie Chapman Catt

Carrie Chapman Catt still supported the League of Women Voters and after W.W.II helped with the United Nations and including women's rights along with Eleanor Roosevelt and Alice Paul to ensure women's rights.

Catt also recognized her alma mater of Iowa State by her donations of money; she was also the first woman to give the commencement address at the college. When she passed on, she donated her entire estate to the college in 1947. The Carrie

Chapman Catt building was built and dedicated in her honor.

Other honors she received being the cover on Time magazine in 1926 and for her achievements was named to the Iowa Hall of Fame in 1975, was inducted into the National Women's in 1982 and in 1992 as one of the ten important Women of the Century.

Getting suffrage and giving women the right to vote had ended up being the main goal for both NAWSA and NWP. Carrie Chapman Catt kept working for women's rights and getting laws passed in their favor, but Alice Paul also worked for these rights. The question was what rights were they seeking? We know that Catt worked for peace, started the League of Women Voters, and women's rights.

Alice Paul was still the leader of the NWP. The party met in 1920 to discuss what their next goal or goals were to be. Most of the women were worn out from working suffrage and retired from the hard work but some such as Lucy Burns, Alva Belmont, Dora Stevens Lewis, Charlotte Perkins Gilman, Crystal Eastman, Florence Kelley, Mabel Vernon, Rheta Childe Dorr and Harriet Stanton Blatch were willing to discuss a future. More women during the latter part of suffrage were entering the job market and wanted equal rights with the men and protection from sex discrimination. They moved to permanent quarters at Sewell House near the Capitol where they started working again. It was renamed the Alva Belmont house who was the primary benefactor; Mabel Vernon was the executive secretary. Alice also had to get rid of a $10,000 debt left over from the suffrage movement.

In the 1920's Alice Paul worked for 600 pieces of legislation at all levels, the local, state, and national. They covered divorce, jury service, property rights, contracts, reinstatement of maiden name after divorce, custody of children and labor legislation. The old NWP was dissolved and a new one opened to achieve the rights but perhaps it was too much diversity as the members and party eventually split into different factions.

Alice Paul had an unfilled mission to see a statue of Lucretia Mott, Elizabeth Stanton, and Susan Anthony placed in the Capitol. It had originally been ordered by NAWSA but had been neglected and forgotten. Ida Husted Harper renewed the interest. When Carrie C Catt rejected the piece, Ida brought it to Alice Paul who took over responsibility and paid Adelaide Johnson $2,000 for the piece. They made plans for the ceremony on February 15, 1921, the anniversary of Susan's birthday. Invitations were sent to every woman's organization dealing with suffrage. There were the business and professional groups including women's clubs, trade unions, housekeepers, Daughters of the Confederacy, Daughters of the American Revolution even the Red Cross. The statute was dedicated to honor these three women suffrage pioneers during the ceremony and was given a permanent placement in the Capitol.

In 1923, Alice Paul along with Crystal Eastman introduced the Lucretia Mott amendment or Equal Rights amendment that included equal pay for all with other items. It was included in every party platform till 1943. Her words" I never doubted that equal rights was the right direction. Most reforms, most problems, are complicated. But to me there is nothing complicated about ordinary equality."[56] It was introduced in every session of Congress and was finally passed in 1972. It has been ratified by thirty-six states (Illinois being the most recent). It was renamed the Alice Paul amendment and is not yet a law.

Alice Paul went on to earn three law degrees LLB, LLIJ, and DCIJ. The first was a law degree; the second was a masters and the third a Doctor of Law. She started the World Peace Party in Geneva, Switzerland in 1938. She worked with the League

---

[56] From Equal Suffrage to Equal Rights, p. 302

of Nations for gender equality and with the United Nations getting women's rights included in the U.N. charter along with Eleanor Roosevelt and Carrie Chapman Catt. Alice Paul was also one of those who were responsible for the Civil Rights Act of 1964. She passed on in 1977 and the Alice Paul Institute of leadership was organized in 1985 for leadership development as a memorial of her work in suffrage.

Just five women started the suffrage movement. By the time the 19th amendment was ratified, two million women were working. All the women who had started the suffrage movement in the early days were not alive when the 19th Amendment was added to the Constitution. All women alive in 1920 when it became law had not been alive in the beginning except for Charlotte Woodward which explains the length of time it took to have suffrage. Rheta Dorr, a member of the NWP party had interviewed her in 1920 about her experiences. Charlotte Woodward Pierce not only signed the Declaration of Rights at Seneca Falls but she worked in suffrage and joined the AWSA group. She knew Lucretia Mott and wrote her explaining about why she had joined the AWSA instead of the NWSA. She even had presented a trowel to the

NWP to lay the cornerstone for its headquarters at Sewell House.

Susan B. Anthony wrote this to Elizabeth Stanton in 1902, "It is fifty-one years since we first met. . .. We little dreamed . . .that half a century later we would be compelled to leave the finish of the battle to another generation of women. But… there is an army of them where we were but a handful."[57] Both Susan Anthony and Elizabeth Cady Stanton believed that suffrage would have been achieved long before it was; in fact they believed it would be done in their lifetime. Alice Paul believed that the Equal Rights Amendment would also have been accepted; yet today it still is not accepted as a law.

There were three hundred people at Seneca Falls with a two -day meeting and little money. By the end of the struggle, over two million women were engaged in the suffrage movement and the conventions lasted six days more each day crowded with meetings, reports, and work having budgets and disbursements of $100,000. First women gave pennies to the movement and then came the thousands. This was accomplished in harmony and respect for each other; they did disagree and squabble over their differences of opinion, but they held to the course of getting suffrage for all women.

[57] Ladies of Seneca Falls, p.302

The story of NAWSA is in the five volumes of The History of Woman Suffrage. Some women didn't care; others were too involved with only their lives and some just didn't know or were too timid to take a stand. Of course, the anti-suffragists were no help at all and joining with the Brewers association was a slam to all women and showed their disdain to all but themselves.

I wanted you to know about their backgrounds and their determination and to recognize and honor these women. They have the right to be respected and able to pursue their career choice. The women were triumphant of earning the right to vote but they soon learned that very little else had changed. The men let them vote but distinctly rejected their equal rights to rule alongside them nor to be members of Congress. It did not guarantee equal pay or equal treatment even to this day.

The 1920's was a time of revolt over old conditions, morals, and attitudes. Women had the vote; they demanded other freedoms from the style of dress to what careers were open to them. The Prohibition amendment was law now too but that did not mean they were denied the right to drink. The alcohol was now made illegally, and crime doubled if not tripled and professional gangsters became a common sight along with the crimes.

I set out to find the solution to my investigation, but I learned so much more. At various times I leaned one way or another but in the final analysis, I saw the value of what all the women had advocated, and I reached the conclusion that all of it was necessary in overcoming the obstacles they faced in this struggle not only the struggles among themselves but the tremendous power and money used to defeat suffrage. It still exists today in other forms which is why there is need for vigilance and continued action against those who would manipulate to achieve their own goals.

I not only researched these women reading again and again to make sure I was as close to the thought projected and their meaning as possible. Researching one woman, I found another one that needed to be researched; I had to review so I was not confusing one woman with another. It has taken me years to do what research I have now. One thing I did not find was that even though women disagreed with other women in their strategies and operation, I did not find vicious attacks on each other or lies about the disagreements that impugned the persons words and yet today this is clearly happening.

The two women who were the most in conflict were Carrie Chapman Catt and Alice Paul over the methods of working for suffrage. Carrie C. Catt believed in getting the amendment in several ways while Alice Paul was adamant on a federal amendment. She only came in 1910 and certainly was aggressive in implementing her ideas. She did not believe that a large organization of committees was necessary to achieve suffrage. This is what she did while in NAWSA taking it upon herself to just charge ahead and use her ideas without asking permission. That's why she was audited but she had spent the money for suffrage. The suffrage parade used to show the suffrage movement was a good idea and brought notice to the suffragists. Blaming the political parties was not such a good idea as she used the idea from England where the Prime Minister and all members of the Parliament were of the same party. Suffering physical abuse after being thrown in jail was hard on the women and especially on Alice Paul who suffered physical problems having been in jail and in later life, she also had relapses of illness from the jail experiences and forced feedings. The way men treated them in jail was a harsh statement of their disregard and brutal treatment of the women. People have different opinions and they come into conflict; no group of people all agree on everything. They realized they both still had the same goal.

The main leaders, Lucretia Mott, Elizabeth Cady Stanton, Susan Anthony, Lucy Stone, and

Alice Paul that I presented along with other unnamed workers worked their entire lives for the suffrage movement. Inez Milholland even died speaking for suffrage and was the first woman to have a memorial service in the Capitol.

Lucretia was the first to say how proud she was of the young suffragists coming up the ranks. Susan Anthony said the same thing and they both felt secure in the knowledge that suffrage would be a viable conclusion in the future.

The struggle is not over by any means; there is much to do. Awareness is one of the key factors of what is occurring. How quickly can laws be changed and rights taking away without any of us being fully alert to what's happening. It has already happened in some instances and it is very ludicrous of us to ignore the warnings and be complacent. One of these concerns is the Equality Act that is proposed in Congress concerning Title IX and transgender applications. It would affect women in many walks of life including sports. Abigail Duniway's quote best sums it up as to what women must do not should do.

"The young college women of today free to study, to speak, to write or to choose their own occupation should remember that every inch of this freedom was bought for them at a great price. It is for them to show their gratitude by helping onward the reforms of their own time by spreading the light of freedom and of truth still wider. The debt that each generation owes to the past must pay to the future."[58]

Elizabeth Cady Stanton in 1899 recognized also the need to pay attention and focus on what needs to be done. "So many of our followers think they do enough if they sing suffrage, which now calls down no ridicule or persecution. But the battle is not wholly fought until we stand equal in the church, the world of work, and have an equal code of morals for both sexes."[59]

Lucy Burns already said it after going through all the forced feedings, treatment, and number of times she served in jail. It bears repeating "I am not going to fight anymore. I think we have done all this for women, and we have sacrificed everything we possessed for them and now let them fight for it now."[60]

And surprise, Charlotte Woodward Pierce, the only surviving woman from Seneca Falls had this to say in her interview with Rheta Dorr. "The NWP

---

[58] A-Z Quotes, Duniway papers Collection 23213, 1852- Wikiquotes

[59] Ladies of Seneca Falls, p. 271

[60] Jailed for Freedom, p. 324, Lunardi quotes

seems to be a woman's party. I do not believe in that. I think women should go into the existing

parties. My heart is with all women who vote. They have gained it now and they should not quarrel about the method of using it."[61]

There is your beginning. You have an idea of what these ladies sacrificed to work for the cause of suffrage. It's not over just continuing. Freedom and rights must be maintained, and it takes each one of us to be vigilant and supportive. We know there are those who will do nothing, but they may complain but they have the choice to get involved. The key words are support and work. You do not have to work full time but stand and work for rights that are important to you. In the last three years, I have seen little but hatred and vicious words spoken to destroy people. If that had been during the suffrage movement, women still would not be able to vote. There are many organizations available for women today that will get you involved and guide you. Many new laws also are on the books that were not there in 1920 or even ten years ago.

---

[61] From Equal Suffrage to Equal Rights, Wikiquotes Interview by Rheta Dorr of Charlotte Woodward Pierce

Make your decision where you want women's rights to be in your lifetime and work for it!

BIBLIOGAPHY

Charging a Hat or Coat

Charging a Hat or Coat

A.A.U.W. www.aauw.org 79 examples of how women are still treated unequally
A.A.U.W. Outlook winter of 2017
Abigail Scott Duniway Papers 1852 Quotes Wikiquotes top 5 quotes
Abram, Ruth Jed Send Us a Lady Physician Women Doctors in America 1835-1920
Atter, Judith Women in the Old West, New e Old West, New York, Franklin Watts, 1989
Andrews, Mildred Tanner, Washington Women as Path Breakers, Dubuque, Ia., Kendall Hunt, 1989
Bacon, Margaret Hope, The Life of Lucretia Mott, NY, 1090
Beach, Cora M. Women of Wyoming, Casper, Wyoming S.F. Boyer, 1927
Berkeley, Ellen Perry,ed. Architecture, A Place for Women, Washington Smithsonian Institution, 1989
B Bkornlund, Lydia   Women of the Suffrage Movement, Thompson Gale Lucent Books, 2003
Buhle, Mary Jo and Paul, Selections from History of Women Suffrage, edited by Elizabeth Cady Stanton, 1978-2005
Blair, Karen ,Women of the Pacific Northwest, History of Seattle, Washington, University of Washingon Press,1988
Boutelle, Sara Holmes, Julia Morgan, Architect, Santa Cruz California, December 10,1990
Buechler, Steven Women's Movements in the U,S,, Woman Suffrage Equal Rights, and Beyond, 1990
Bushman, Claudia, Mormon Sisters in early Utah, Salt Lake City, Utah
Catt, Carrie C, Nellie Rogers Schuler, Woman Suffrage and Politics, the inner story of the suffrage movement, Seattle and London, University of Washington Press, 1923-6
Carter, Jimmy, A Call to Action, Simon and Schuster, N.Y.,2014
Clark, Bob, Interview on Woman Suffrage in Montana Helena, Montana, Historical Society May 13, 1990
Dobler, Lavina, Esther Morris First Woman Justice of the Peace, Riverton, Wyoming, Big Bend Press, 1993
Dorough, Jeff C., Dorough, Joe D.,Dorough, Marybeth, Women Of The West, Volume I and II,1992 by Dorough Enterprises
Duniway, Abigail Path Breaking a Biogtaphy History, 1914
Edwards, G. Thomas, Sowing Good Seeds, Portland, Oregon, Historical Society,1989
G.Garrard, Bennett, Wayne, Women Who Dared to be Different, editing Commentary Publishing
Gurko, Miriam, Ladies of Seneca Falls, Schoeken Books, NY 1974
Gurley, Catherine, Gibson Girls and Suffragists, Twenty-first Century Books, 2008 Minneapolis, Minnesota
Gilbert, Peggy, Laura de Force Gordon Activist, Journalist, Lawyer, Research Paper, Lodi,California
Heidt, Maryann, Fighting for Equal Rights, about Susan B. Anthony, Carolrodha Books Inc. Minneapolis, Minnesota, 2004

History of Woman Suffrage in six volumes, Volume 1-1848-186l appeared in 1881; v.2-1861-1876 1876 appeared in 1882; v. 3 1876-1885 appeared in 1886. These three volumes were written and and edited by Elizabeth Cady Stanton, Susan B. Anthony, and Matilda Joslyn Gage. Ayer Co. Publishers, Salem, New Hampshire, 1885
History of Woman Suffrage Suffrage v.4 1883-1900, Edited by Susan B. Anthony and Ida Husted, Harper Ayer Publishers, Salem, New Hampshire, Reprint, 1985

History of Woman Suffrage volumes 5 and 6 printed by the National American Womens Suffrage Association, 1922

Holmes, Kenneth L. and Duniway, David, Covered Wagon Women, Diaries and Letters

Housley, Kathleen L. The Letter but the Spirit Gives Life: The Smiths Abolitionists, Suffragists Bible Translators, Glastonberry, Ct. :Historical Society of Glastonbury, 1993 From Western Trails-1840-1890, Glendale, California, Arthur Clark Co.

James, Cary Julia Morgan, Chelsea House Publishers, N.Y. 1990

Jeffrey, Julie Ray, Frontier Women, the trail west-1840-1880, N.Y., Hill and Wang,1981

Jewish Women's Archive, Ernestine Rose presides over NAWSA convention, 1854 Https// jwd.org10/19

Jerrido, Margaret, Interviews on Pioneer Women Doctors Medical Collection-Penn. 12/1/1969

Kuclnd, Gerald, Early Leaders of the Women's Liberation Movement.1972 Story House Corp. Charlottesville, N.Y. Sanbar Press

Library of Congress Link Sojourner Truth's speech Aint I Woman by Marcus Robinson Anti-Slavery Bugle 1851

Lunardi, Christine, From Equal Suffrage to Equal Rights, 1910-1928, NY University Press, 1986 ,(Alice Paul-NWP)

Massie, Michael A., "Reform is where you find it", Annals of Wy, Spring, 1990 pgs.3-21 Esther Morris

McHenry, Robert, Fammous American Women ,NY Dover Publications Inc., 1980

Michaels, Debra "Carrie Chapman Catt" National Women's History Museum 6/17/2019 www.women'shistory.org/education resources/biographies/Carrie Chapman Catt

Moynihan, Ruth B., Rebel For Rights: Duniway, New Haven, Yale Press, 1983

Morgan, David, Suffragists and Democrats The Politics of Woman Suffrage in America, 1972 Michigan State University Press

Morrison, Dorothy Nafus, Ladies Were Not Expected, Salem, Or. Western Imprint, 1985

Palas, Nicholas C., "San Diego's Portia of the Pacific" California's First Woman Lawyer The Journal of San Diego: pgs.m185-195, 1980

Stanton, Elizabeth Cady, Eighty Years and More, Reminiscenes, Intro by Gail Parker, Schoeken Books, NY,1889

Stanton, Theodore and Stanton, Harriet (Blatch), Elizabeth Cady Stanton as Revealed in Her Letters, Diary, and Reminiscenes Vol 1 & 2, Harper Bros., 1922

Stevens, Doris, Jailed For Freedom, Liverwright, NY., 1920

S. Sterling , Dorothy, Lucretia Mott Gentle Warrior, Doubleday and Co. Inc. Garden City, NY.   1898

Weidt, Morgan, Fighting for Equal Rights (about Susan Anthony) Carolhoa Books Inc., Minneapolis, Mn., 2004

Whitney, Sharon, The Equal Rights Amendment, the history and the movement, NY, London, Franklin Watts, 1984

ABOUT THE AUTHOR

Jean Lane is a former history teacher in Decatur, IL. Upon retiring after 30 years of teaching, she began an in-depth research of women, especially their efforts in obtaining voting rights, which is suffrage. Charging a hat or coat relates this story and its long journey toward success.
The 19th Amendment was declared law on August 18, 1920.

Charging a Hat or Coat

Made in the USA
Monee, IL
08 October 2020